THE
NATURALIST'S
HANDBOOK

HOW TO FIND, WATCH AND STUDY WILD FLOWERS, BIRDS AND OTHER WILDLIFE

AUTHORS
Ros Evans, Ian Wallace, Andrew Cooper

ILLUSTRATORS
Victoria Goaman, Alan Harris, Ian Jackson, Janet Blakeley/Middletons.

EDITORS
Karen Goaman, Rick Morris, Martyn Bramwell

DESIGNERS
Caroline Hill, Karen Goaman

ADDITIONAL ILLUSTRATIONS
Julie Piper, John Sibbick, Will Giles, Sally Burrough, David Hurrell/Middletons,
Andrew Ingram, Sheila Galbraith.

PHOTOGRAPHS
David Ridge, Geoffrey Kinns, Michael Chinery

THE EDITORS WISH TO THANK THE FOLLOWING PEOPLE FOR THEIR HELP
Colin and Peggy Legg, Hilary Scott, David Beeson

CONTENTS

First published in 1982 by Usborne Publishing Limited, 20 Garrick Street, London WC2E 9BJ

© 1982 Usborne Publishing Limited

The name Usborne and the device 🐝 are Trade Marks of Usborne Publishing Limited

Printed in Scotland by Blantyre Printing & Binding Company Limited

UNDERSTANDING
WILD
FLOWERS

INTRODUCTION

Wherever you go, the countryside is covered with plants of various shapes and sizes. The most successful and dominant of these are the flowering plants and, without them, all other forms of life on earth today would not exist.

When these plants bloom, they provide a beautiful range of countless colours, shapes and scents. The flower represents a very important stage in the life cycle of these plants, since it is through the flower that each generation begins.

How to use this section
The first part of this section concentrates on the flower and its purpose and why there are so many different designs even though they all have the same purpose – to reproduce the species.

The second part, "Flower Families", may help to explain some of the similarities you may notice between certain flowers. The descriptions of families, and in particular the key on pages 32–4, should give you a short cut to identifying a flower.

You will probably have noticed some of the characteristic flowers of certain habitats – for instance the primroses and bluebells which carpet the woodland floors in spring. The third part, "Flower Habitats", considers the characteristic flowers which you could look out for in different kinds of places (habitats), and begins to answer the question of why they have chosen to grow in these places rather than others.

As you get to know more about flowers, you may want to make closer observations out in the countryside. There are some suggestions for ways of looking at flowers and recording what you see on pages 58–9.

If you come across a term you do not understand in this section, look it up in the index. It may have been explained earlier in the section, usually on the first page listed in the index.

▼ **Purple loosestrife, meadowsweet and hemlock may be found beside rivers and streams.**

THE PURPOSE OF FLOWERS
Parts of a flower

The flower is the centre of a flowering plant's sex life. The flower contains the male and female sex organs, which produce the sex cells. When these fuse, a seed forms and a new generation begins.

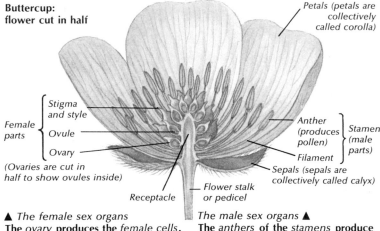

**Buttercup:
flower cut in half**

Petals (petals are collectively called corolla)

Female parts {
Stigma and style
Ovule
Ovary
}
(Ovaries are cut in half to show ovules inside)

Anther (produces pollen)
Filament
} Stamen (male parts)

Sepals (sepals are collectively called calyx)

Receptacle

Flower stalk or pedicel

▲ The female sex organs
The ovary produces the female cells. The ovary also encloses the cells to protect them.

The male sex organs ▲
The anthers of the stamens produce the male cells, each one protected in a pollen grain.

From flower to fruit
In all flowers, it is the ovary which develops into a fruit containing one or more seeds. The male and female cells of the same or different plants of the same species must fuse in order to produce a seed. The fusion is called fertilization (see page 8). For fertilization to occur, pollen must first be transferred from the anther of a stamen (male) to the stigma of an ovary (female). This process is called pollination. Pollination may be carried out by the wind, or by insects visiting the flower in search of food (see pages 9–14).

Buttercup: after fertilization

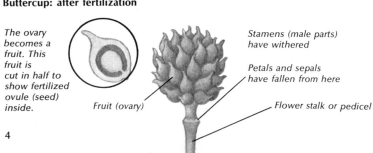

The ovary becomes a fruit. This fruit is cut in half to show fertilized ovule (seed) inside.

Fruit (ovary)

Stamens (male parts) have withered

Petals and sepals have fallen from here

Flower stalk or pedicel

Parts of a flower and their functions
Although sexual reproduction is the main function of all flowers, in many, the sexual organs (stamens and ovaries) are hardly noticeable. This is because the other parts of the flower take on the role of protecting the sexual organs and of attracting insects to visit them, so that pollination is carried out.

The *sepals* (collectively called the *calyx*) are usually small and green and are sometimes fused together. Their main purpose is to protect the flower while it is in bud.

The *petals* (collectively called the *corolla*) are often fused together. They are usually large and attractive in shape, colour and scent, in order to advertise the flower to insect-pollinators. The petals often pro-duce nectar, a sweet liquid which insects love to drink. Nectaries – the glands which produce nectar – are sometimes found on the receptacle or other parts of the flower instead.

Occasionally the sepals are the attractive parts. The petals can then concentrate on nectar production (see winter aconite below).

Numbers of ovaries and ovules
In some plants like the buttercup and bramble, the flowers have several ovaries, each with a single ovule. In others such as lupin, the flower contains a single ovary with several ovules, each of which, once fertilized, develops into a seed. In some species such as bellflower, the ovaries are fused together (see below).

▼ Petals often produce nectar, the sweet liquid attractive to insects.

Buttercup petal

Nectary, which produces the sweet liquid called nectar

▼ In some flowers the sepals instead of the petals are coloured. Winter aconite has shiny yellow sepals which serve to attract insects, and the petals are tubular nectaries.

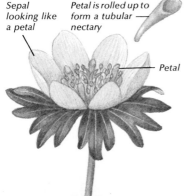

Sepal looking like a petal

Petal is rolled up to form a tubular nectary

Petal

▼ Lupin flower, cut in half, showing the single ovary containing several ovules.

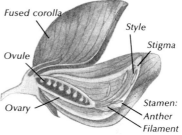

Fused corolla

Style

Stigma

Ovule

Ovary

Stamen:
Anther
Filament

▼ Bellflower, cut in half, showing ovaries and styles fused together.

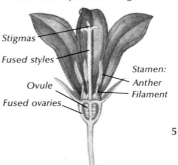

Stigmas

Fused styles

Ovule

Fused ovaries

Stamen:
Anther
Filament

5

Inflorescences

Surprisingly enough, very few plants bear single flowers. Most flowers are borne in a characteristic arrangement or *inflorescence*. This may look haphazard but in fact each species always sticks to its own pattern of inflorescence, which has a particular purpose. All types of inflorescence have the same aims – to hold the flowers in the most suitable position for pollination and for seed dispersal, and to extend the flowering period.

Once you start looking at inflorescences, you will find a great variety from species to species, and yet some interesting similarities between species even of different families. When you are trying to identify a flower, it is helpful to draw the type of inflorescence as well as the flower. The most common types of inflorescence are shown on these two pages.

(Note: *Peduncle* means the stalk which bears the whole inflorescence. *Pedicel* means the stalk which bears the single flower.)

Raceme

▲ One type of inflorescence is the *raceme*. The flowers, each on its own pedicel, occur at intervals in a spiral up the peduncle. The foxglove above is an example of a raceme. A catkin is also a raceme, often hanging upside down.

▼ One of the most confusing inflorescences is the *head* or *capitulum*. The clustering of flowers together looks just like a single flower. In fact, as shown in the magnifying glass below, the flower head is made up of hundreds of tiny flowers. Each single flower is equipped with its own male and female sexual organs and each is capable of producing a seed.

Most members of the daisy family (Compositae), like the ox-eye daisy shown below, have this type of inflorescence.

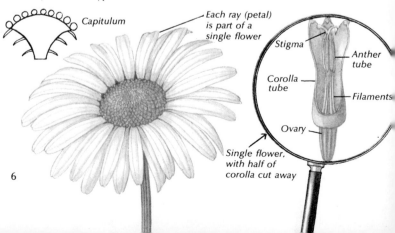

Capitulum

Each ray (petal) is part of a single flower

Stigma

Anther tube

Corolla tube

Filaments

Ovary

Single flower, with half of corolla cut away

6

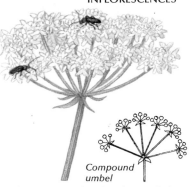

Umbel

▲ In some flowers all the pedicels grow from the tip of the peduncle. This forms a cluster which may be held up, as in ramsons, or droop, as in cowslip above. This type of inflorescence is called an *umbel*.

Compound umbel

▲ The cow parsley family (Umbelliferae) bear *compound umbels*. This is really an umbel of umbels (see cowslips), since the peduncle branches before bearing umbels. The umbels are often flat-topped to provide a platform for insect-pollinators to land on. Some insects also use the platform as a place to display to attract mates, like the soldier beetles on the hogweed above.

▼ Another type of inflorescence is the *cyme*. Here, instead of pedicels growing from the peduncle, the peduncle itself produces a flower so it cannot grow any further. The side branches therefore carry on the growth. But they too end in flowers so *their* side branches must continue the growth.

The red campion (left) is a common example of a cyme. In the forget-me-not (right), the inflorescence starts with two side branches just as in red campion. From then on there is only one side branch each time, and it is always produced on the same side, so the inflorescence stalk becomes coiled.

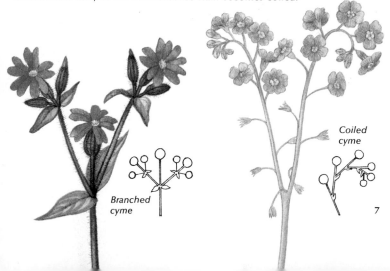

Coiled cyme

Branched cyme

7

Sexual reproduction

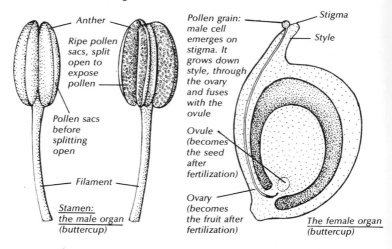

Anther

Ripe pollen sacs, split open to expose pollen

Pollen sacs before splitting open

Filament

Stamen: the male organ (buttercup)

Pollen grain: male cell emerges on stigma. It grows down style, through the ovary and fuses with the ovule

Stigma

Style

Ovule (becomes the seed after fertilization)

Ovary (becomes the fruit after fertilization)

The female organ (buttercup)

▲ Before fertilization can take place – that is the fusing together of male and female cells – the pollen grain must first be transferred from the male anther to the receptive *stigma* of a female ovary. This process is called *pollination*.

The male cell emerges from the pollen grain on the surface of the stigma, and penetrates the ovary wall. It passes down through the style to the ovule, where it fuses with the female cell. This process is called *fertilization*.

But remember that only pollen from the same species will be "compatible" – able to grow down through the stigma and ovary and fertilize the ovule.

The purpose of flowers is to produce seeds from which a new generation will grow.

Before a seed can form, a flower must be fertilized (see caption to illustration above). But first of all, pollination must take place – pollen must be transferred from the anther (male) to the stigma (female), usually in the flower of another plant.

Different types of pollination
Most flowering plants are *hermaphrodite*, that is they produce both male and female sexual organs in the same flower. So pollen does not have far to travel to reach the female stigma in the same flower. If this happens, it is called *self-pollination*.

However, since the male cell is protected in a pollen grain, it can be transported by wind or by insects over long distances. If pollen reaches the stigma of a flower on another plant, *cross-pollination* will have occurred. The male cell is therefore able to fertilize different plants of the same species – a process called *cross-fertilization*.

In fact, it is far more usual for cross-fertilization to take place, even though most flowers are hermaphrodite. The reasons for this are discussed on page 15.

Pollination

Different methods of pollination

In Europe, flowers are pollinated mainly by *wind* or by *insects*. The same is true in other temperate, Mediterranean and arctic regions of the world. Other animals may sometimes act as pollinators, but this is more common in tropical regions, where birds and bats are important pollinators.

Insect-pollinated flowers are usually colourful, scented and often produce nectar. *Wind-pollinated* flowers tend to be less colourful, often green, with no scent or nectar. Read on for further differences.

Insect-pollination (or entomophilly)

Insect-pollinated flowers usually have a large, colourful, scented corolla (or calyx) which makes them attractive to insects. Insects come to expect some kind of reward when they visit an attractive flower. The reward may be in the form of nectar,

▼ Grasses, like all wind-pollinated flowers, have no need for petals, scent or nectar. Their anthers and stigmas hang outside the flower so pollen is freely released into the wind or picked up from it.

the sweet liquid produced by the nectary, or pollen which is also a nutritious foodstuff for insects. Some flowers such as poppy do not produce nectar and must entice insects by their pollen alone. These flowers produce an abundance of pollen so as to leave some spare for reproductive purposes.

While seeking nectar or collecting pollen from a flower, an insect's body may brush against the stamens and pick up pollen from the anthers. Its pollen-covered body may then contact the stigmas and leave pollen on them.

If the pollen comes from anthers of the same plant then self-pollination will have been carried out. If the pollen came from another plant then cross-pollination will have been achieved.

The pollen

The surface of the entomophillous pollen grain must be sticky or rough in order to adhere to the insect-pollinator's body.

▼ Insect-pollinated flowers have showy petals, and often produce scent and nectar. Some flowers like the poppy have no nectar so must entice insects with their pollen alone. They therefore have lots of stamens to produce abundant pollen.

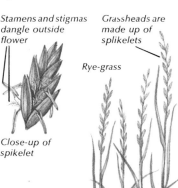

Stamens and stigmas dangle outside flower

Grassheads are made up of splikelets

Rye-grass

Close-up of spikelet

9

Colour and pattern

Most insects do not see colours in the same way that people do, but they can see bluish colours as we see them. Because of this, in temperate regions where insects are the chief pollinators to be attracted, a large proportion of flowers are blue.

Insects are also sensitive to ultraviolet rays, invisible to us, which are reflected from the surface of the petals of some flowers. So they see on petals patterns which our eyes cannot detect.

In the tropics, where birds are also important pollinators, there are just as many red flowers as' blue ones. This is because birds have the same colour vision as people.

Many petals bear patterns, markings or colour changes, often in ultra-violet wavelengths visible only to insects. These patterns tend to draw the eye towards the centre of the flower. They act as guidelines to the insects, pointing to the nectar and leading the insects into contact with anther and stigma.

▼ Sea bindweed attracts insects with its trumpet-shaped flowers, and then "leads" the insect into the source of nectar with its pink and white stripes. The pink stripes are scented differently from the white stripes too.

Mature flowers are blue

Buds are pinky-red

▲ In comfrey the flowers are pinky-red in bud and then slowly turn through mauve to blue when they are mature and rich in nectar. Bees are more sensitive to blue than red and will therefore visit the more mature flowers in favour of those which have just opened. The change in colour indicates that they are ready to be pollinated.

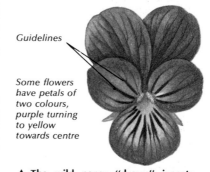

Guidelines

Some flowers have petals of two colours, purple turning to yellow towards centre

▲ The wild pansy "draws" insects inside the flower with its dark stripes.

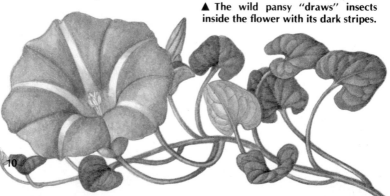

Flower scents

The overall scent of a flower is in fact the combination of many different scents produced from the surface of the petal. In most flowers the scent changes and becomes stronger towards the base of each petal. Insects therefore have yet another guideline to draw them into the centre of the flower.

Nectar

The nectar of open flowers such as dogrose is contained in shallow pools accessible to any type of insect which visits. But many flowers provide nectar in a reservoir, formed simply by the petals fusing together into a corolla tube.

In some flowers the corolla is extended into spurs, as in toadflax, or pouches, as in snapdragon. Spurs and pouches can contain a large quantity of nectar, and the design of the flower means that only certain insects, for example bees with long tongues, can reach the nectar. This ensures that the correct insect-pollinator visits the flower. The insect, richly rewarded with a large store of nectar, then looks for another flower of the same species. This increases the chances of successful cross-pollination.

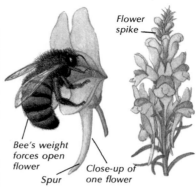

Flower spike

Bee's weight forces open flower

Spur

Close-up of one flower

▲ **Toadflax stores its nectar for the right pollinator by closing the mouth of the corolla. Only the larger bees are heavy enough to open the mouth and obtain the nectar inside the spur – formed of the corolla tube. The nectar is inaccessible to smaller insects whose bodies would be too small to brush against anthers and stigma efficiently.**

▼ **The honeysuckle is pollinated chiefly by moths. It has two devices to attract moths. Firstly, its scent is stronger at night when moths are most active. Secondly, it produces a deep supply of nectar at the end of a long corolla tube, which is only accessible to long-tongued insects.**

Whole flowerhead

Butterflies and moths, can obtain the nectar with their long probosces "tongues"

Single flower

11

Singling out the right pollinator

Primitive flowers (see page 28) such as buttercup and poppy attract, indiscriminately, insects which may have previously visited all kinds of different species. These flowers must produce a large quantity of pollen with their numerous stamens in order to increase the chances of at least some pollen reaching the stigma of the same species. So a lot of pollen is wasted.

The more advanced "closed" flowers can be more economical in their production of pollen since they are designed to attract a single customer. They are pollinated efficiently by one or just a few species of insects which are likely to seek out the same flowers. These more advanced flowers may bear as few as one stamen (see Orchids page 38). The more advanced flowers must have features which prevent pollen or nectar being "stolen" by the wrong species.

Some insects are so tiny that, although they are unable to reach the nectar with their tongues, they may be able to climb down to the nectar source without touching either anther or stigma. Some flowers such as foxglove bar the way to the tiny insects with a battery of hairs. Others such as toadflax shown on page 11 have a closed mouth to the corolla tube. In both cases, only the larger beasts are undeterred and barge their way through, brushing against the anther and stigma.

Teasels prevent ants from reaching▶ the flowers by catching pools of water in their cupped leaves. Ants are unsuitable as pollinators for most flowers since they are too small and smooth for pollen to stick to their bodies.

▼ The foxglove has a battery of hairs inside its corolla tube. This prevents small insects who would be inefficient pollinators from entering the flower and taking the nectar, since they would get tangled up in the hairs.

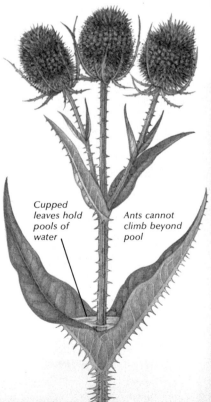

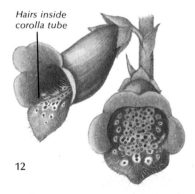

Hairs inside
corolla tube

Cupped
leaves hold
pools of
water

Ants cannot
climb beyond
pool

Wind-pollination (or anemophilly)

Not all flowers are the colourful, showy ones designed to attract insect-pollinators. Flowers which are pollinated by wind have no need for such attractiveness.

Features of wind-pollinated flowers

Wind-pollinated (or anemophillous) flowers are small and inconspicuous and consist mainly of reproductive organs. Grasses, sedges, rushes and most catkin-bearing trees are pollinated by wind. But there are other examples from other families of flowering plants, for instance salad burnet in the rose family, and meadow rue in the buttercup family. In all cases, the inflorescences can be very attractive, but the individual flowers are small and unshowy.

Notice how the anthers are borne on very long filaments and dangle and shake in the wind. A showy display of petals would prevent them moving freely in the wind.

The stigmas of wind-pollinated flowers are usually larger and more feathery than those of insect-pollinated flowers. They are designed to trap pollen grains passing in the wind, unobstructed by a corolla. As in insect-pollinated flowers, only pollen from the same species will be compatible.

The pollen

Anemophillous (wind-borne) pollen grains tend to be smaller and lighter than entomophillous ones. They are therefore more easily transported by slight air currents.

Hazel catkins flower from January to March. All catkins appear early in the year, before the trees' foliage develops and hinders the exchange of pollen in the wind. Like all wind-pollinated flowers, the individual flowers are small and unshowy, though as may be seen here, the inflorescences can be very attractive.

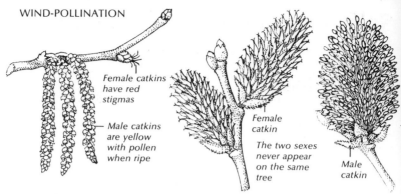

Female catkins have red stigmas

Male catkins are yellow with pollen when ripe

Female catkin

The two sexes never appear on the same tree

Male catkin

▲ Hazel is a monoecious plant – that is one which bears unisexual flowers, either completely male or completely female, on the same plant. Notice how different the male and female catkins are in appearance.

Types of sexuality

Wind-pollinated flowers are often *unisexual* (containing either just male or just female parts) rather than *hermaphrodite* (containing both). Catkin-bearing trees, for example, all have unisexual flowers. The female flowers are gathered into female catkins and the male ones into male catkins.

Sometimes the same plant bears both male and female catkins. Hazel is an example of this.

In other species, for example all the willows, each plant bears either all male or all female catkins.

Hazel then is called *monoecious* (meaning *one* home for both sexes) and willow is called *dioecious* (meaning *two* homes, one for the male and one for the female). Dioecism makes self-pollination impossible, so cross-pollination is necessary if fertilization is to take place. Cross-pollination is more common anyway, whether a plant is unisexual or hermaphrodite (see pages 15–18).

▲ Willows are dioecious plants – meaning that each plant bears either all male or all female flowers. Willow catkins are pollinated both by wind and by insects, since, though there is no showy corolla, willow catkins do produce nectar.

The world distribution of wind- and insect-pollinated plants

Flowering plants are thought to have originated in tropical climates. In the humid atmosphere of the tropical rain forest there are few breezes let alone wind, so most flowers are pollinated by insects and birds.

In contrast, in the more severe regions of the world – in the arctic and in areas at high altitude – the plants that can survive are mainly wind-pollinated. It would seem therefore that these plants have adapted to these grim regions by developing features to cope with the conditions. Since there are comparatively few insects around, but an unlimited supply of relentless wind, flowers have evolved features to use the wind to pollinate them.

Wind-pollinated flowers are therefore thought to have evolved from insect-pollinated ones, spreading outwards from the tropics where flowering plants are most likely to have originated.

Self- versus cross-pollination

Most flowers are capable of self-pollination, since they contain both male and female parts. However, though self-fertilization is not harmful, if it takes place repeatedly over a few generations of plants, it may not do the species much good (but see page 18 and also "Wasteland weeds" pages 42–43).

Disadvantages of self-fertilization

Seeds produced by self-fertilization (that is fusion between male and female sex cells from the *same* plant) will grow into offspring which are almost identical to the parent plant.

The new generation will probably be ideally suited to the habitat in which the parent is growing. But there will not be much variation amongst all the different offspring, and they will therefore be less adaptable to new places or to the parent's habitat if it should change a great deal.

Another possible disadvantage of self-fertilization is that undesirable characteristics may be passed on to the next generation. If self-fertilization takes place repeatedly over a few generations, these characteristics may become exaggerated.

Advantages of cross-fertilization

If cross-fertilization takes place (that is the fusion of male and female sex cells from *different* plants), the offspring produced will have a number of characteristics different from either of the parents. So at least some of them will be more likely to conquer new places, or even different types of habitat, or survive in the parents' habitat if it should alter.

Because of the disadvantages of self-fertilization, most plants have features to favour cross-fertilization.

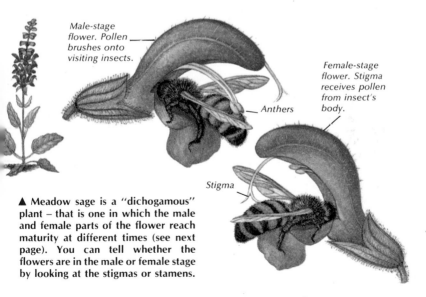

Male-stage flower. Pollen brushes onto visiting insects.

Female-stage flower. Stigma receives pollen from insect's body.

— *Anthers*

Stigma

▲ Meadow sage is a "dichogamous" plant – that is one in which the male and female parts of the flower reach maturity at different times (see next page). You can tell whether the flowers are in the male or female stage by looking at the stigmas or stamens.

Staggered development

Self-pollination is less likely to occur when the male and female parts of the flower reach maturity at different times. This is called "dichogamy", and plants in which this happens are said to be "dichogamous". Either the stigma becomes receptive to pollen only after the pollen-bearing anthers have withered; or the stigma may mature before the stamens and anthers. Therefore pollination will result only if pollen has been received from another flower. The flower will generally be on another plant, so cross-pollination results.

Dichogamy, however does not entirely eliminate the risk of self-pollination. Rosebay willowherb is a common example of a dichogamous plant. Like many other species, this plant has a raceme of several flowers, which open in sequence over several weeks. This means that flowers on the same plant will be at different stages of maturity. Pollen could easily pass from a "male-stage" flower to a "female-stage" flower on the same plant, risking in-breeding.

In fact, self-pollination seldom occurs because the flowers open from the bottom of the plant upwards. Bees tend to visit the lowermost flowers first, and work their way up the plant. So they will visit the more mature (female-stage) flowers first, and the pollen-bearing (male-stage) flowers afterwards.

Rosebay willowherb is another ▶ "dichogamous" plant. The more mature flowers in the female stage tend to be lower down the plant, and bees will visit these first. So pollen is likely to be transferred to *another* plant.

Flowers of different sexes on the same plant

Another way in which plants may restrict self-fertilization is by monoecism. A monoecious plant produces two types of flowers – male flowers which develop only stamens, and female flowers in which ovaries develop but no stamens. Many trees, for example birch and hazel (see page 14), are monoecious.

But, like the dichogamous rosebay willowherb, pollen can still be transferred from one flower to another on the same plant, but the chances of self-pollination occurring are reduced.

Male-stage flower – ripe stamens, stigma not yet forked

Female-stage flower – anthers withered, stigma forked ready to receive pollen

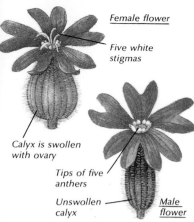

Female flower

Five white
stigmas

Calyx is swollen
with ovary

Tips of five
anthers

Unswollen
calyx

*Male
flower*

▲ **Red campion is a "dioecious" plant, each plant producing either all male or all female flowers. Look for stigmas or stamens, or squeeze the calyx gently, to find out whether a flower is male or female.**

Flowers of one sex only on each plant
Certain species avoid self-pollination in another way: each plant bears either all female or all male flowers. This is called "dioecism". Many plants of the Silene genus (campions and catchflies) and many trees, such as the willows, are dioecious (see page 14).

It is easy to tell if the flower of a dioecious plant, such as red campion, is male or female. Look into the mouth of the corolla to see if stamens or stigmas are emerging. Or squeeze the calyx gently to see if you can feel a swelling – this will be the fruit developing from a fertilized ovary of a female flower.

The problem with dioecism is that, though it ensures cross-pollination, it makes self-pollination impossible. So if during bad weather insect-pollinators are scarce, no seed may be set at all. Some species which are dioecious in mild climates, are only

partly dioecious in severe climates.

For instance, moss campion, which grows on mountains and sea cliffs, is dioecious in the Pyrenees. In the Arctic, however, many plants of this species bear hermaphrodite (male and female) flowers. In Britain, with its relatively mild climate, the species is not completely dioecious, but fewer plants bear hermaphrodite flowers than they do in the Arctic.

Stigmas which prevent self-pollination
Some plants can prevent self-fertilization altogether by producing pollen which is not compatible with the stigmas of the same plant, in the same way that pollen and stigmas are incompatible between different plant species. So only pollen from another plant (of the same species) is able to penetrate the ovary wall. This feature is called *self-incompatibility*.

Some species which have this feature show outward signs of it. For instance the primrose produces two types of plants – one with "pin-eyed" flowers and one with

▼ **The primrose prevents self-pollination by producing two types of plants – one with pin-eyed and one with thrum-eyed flowers. The pollen of one type is not compatible with the other type.**

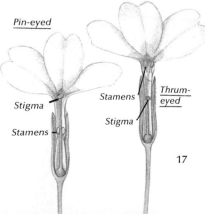

Pin-eyed

Stigma

Stamens

Stamens

Thrum-eyed

Stigma

"thrum-eyed" flowers. Pollen from a pin-eyed plant is incompatible not only with its own stigma but also with the stigmas of all other pin-eyed plants, and vice-versa with thrum-eyed plants. So cross-pollination, from pin-eyed to thrum-eyed flowers or vice-versa, is ensured. You can see the difference between the two types by looking at the flower centres (see page 17). Look at a bank of primroses and try to work out the proportion of each type – there should be about half and half.

Self-pollination as a preference or as a last resort

Some species have features to ensure self-pollination if cross-pollination has not taken place towards the end of the flowering period. Examples of this include violets, honeysuckle and members of the daisy family (Compositae).

Other species can produce seeds without fertilization taking place at all. This is called *apomyxis*. Offspring are identical to the parent plant, so in this way apomyxis is similar to vegetative reproduction (see page 26).

Both these types of plants may risk the disadvantages of self-pollination if it is repeated over several generations. But reproduction is at least ensured, and in some cases this is more important than producing variations in the offspring (see "Wasteland weeds" pages 42–43).

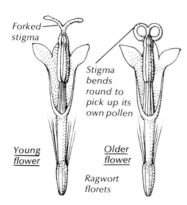

Forked stigma

Stigma bends round to pick up its own pollen

Young flower

Older flower

Ragwort florets

◄ Towards the end of their flowering period, daisy flowers make sure that self-pollination takes place if cross-pollination has failed: the stigma bends down to pick up pollen from the anthers of the same flowers.

▼ Honeysuckle flowers can be seen towards the end of the flowering period with their stigma drooping down, to pick up their own pollen.

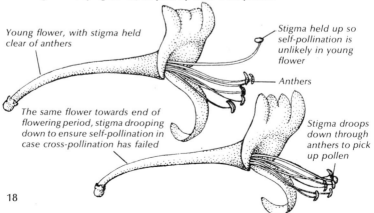

Young flower, with stigma held clear of anthers

Stigma held up so self-pollination is unlikely in young flower

Anthers

The same flower towards end of flowering period, stigma drooping down to ensure self-pollination in case cross-pollination has failed

Stigma droops down through anthers to pick up pollen

Fruits and seeds

From flower to fruit (in poppy)

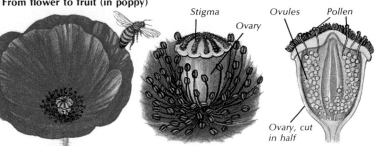

Stigma
Ovary
Ovules   *Pollen*

Ovary, cut in half

1. Pollination: Pollen from one flower is left on the stigma of another by a visiting bee.

2. The male cell emerges from the pollen grain and grows down inside the ovary, which contains many ovules.

3. Fertilization: On reaching an ovule, the male cell fuses with the female cell of the ovule.

6. Seed dispersal: When the fruit ripens, holes form in the top, so when the fruit is shaken in the wind, seeds fall out and are blown away from the parent plant.

4. The fertilized ovules begin to develop into seeds. The petals and stamens die and fall.

5. The ovaries swell and develop into a fruit containing the seeds.

The purpose of flowers and fruits

At the end of the flowering season, the plant world becomes festooned with a mass of fruits of different shapes, sizes, colours and textures. They have all developed from successful flowers.

The **purpose of flowers** is to produce seeds from fertilized ovules in the ovary. The petals start to wither, since they have finished their task of attracting insect-pollinators. At the same time the ovary wall begins to develop into a fruit.

The **purpose of fruits**, whatever their structure, is to ensure that seeds are dispersed – distributed away from the parent plant. This gives the seedlings a chance to develop without too much competition from other plants of the same species.

19

Different methods of seed dispersal
Seeds may be carried to different places in a variety of ways, but the commonest methods are by *wind*, by *animals* (either on their fur or through their droppings), by *explosion* of the fruit, or, in the case of many aquatic plants, by *water*.

By wind. Many plants bear fruits with features which enable them to become airborne.

By animals. Succulent fruits may be eaten by animals. The seeds are not digested but pass out in the droppings.
   Some fruits have hooks or prickles so that they catch on to the coats of passing animals, and drop off later onto "new" soil.

By explosion. Some fruits explode when ripe so the seeds inside are scattered away from the parent plant.

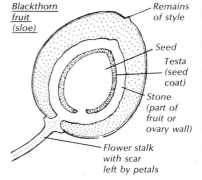

Different types of fruits
The fruits that first spring to mind are *succulent* (juicy) fruits like oranges and plums. The different forms of succulent fruits are shown below and opposite. Overleaf the various types of *dry* fruits, like acorns and pea pods, are described.

Succulent fruits

The sweet juicy flesh of succulent fruits is an important source of food for animals, especially birds. Often the whole fruit is eaten – seeds and all. The seeds are not digested and are passed out in the animals' droppings, often quite far away from the parent plant. Some seeds cannot germinate unless they are first activated by an animal's digestive juices.

Drupes ▶
The fruit (called a sloe) of the blackthorn bush has a hard centre or stone which contains the seed. The fruit develops from a flower which blossomed several months before. The flower had a *single ovary* containing just one ovule or seed. This type of fruit is called a *drupe*.

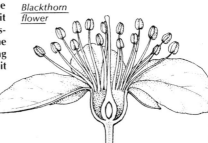

Blackthorn fruit (sloe) — Remains of style / Seed / Testa (seed coat) / Stone (part of fruit or ovary wall) / Flower stalk with scar left by petals

Blackthorn flower

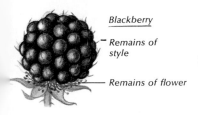

Blackberry

— *Remains of style*

— *Remains of flower*

Remains of flower

Fleshy receptacle

Seed (ovule)

Flower stalk

Rosehip

Core – ovary with seeds

Fleshy receptacle

Apple

Remains of flower

Seed (pip)

Flower stalk

Core – ovary with seeds

Drupules ▲

The blackberry fruit of bramble bushes consists of a collection of drupes called *drupules*. Each drupule is similar in structure to the blackthorn sloe. If you look closely at a blackberry, especially an unripe one, you can still see the remains of the style attached to the top of each ovary. If you compare this to a flower which is still in bloom, you can, with the aid of a magnifying glass, see the tiny ovaries waiting to be pollinated. Once fertilized, they will swell up into succulent drupules.

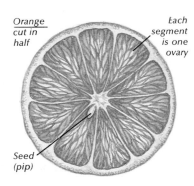

Orange cut in half

Each segment is one ovary

Seed (pip)

Berries ▲

The succulent fruits of orange trees and tomato plants are technically called *berries*. This is because they are made up of *more than one ovary fused together*. (In bramble for instance the ovaries are not fused to each other.) In the orange, illustrated above, each segment is formed from one of the ovaries making up the whole fruit.

False fruits ▲

Rosehips and apples are not like drupes and berries. This is because the true fruit is in fact the core, which consists of the ovaries. The whole is called a false fruit because the fleshy part is not part of the ovary: it is the swollen top of the flower stalk – the receptacle. The fleshy portion has enveloped the true fruit.

Dry fruits

There are two ways in which dry fruits help seeds to be scattered. Either the whole fruit is formed with features to aid dispersal, or else it bursts open while still attached to the plant, so the seeds are catapulted clear of their parent. Fruits which burst open are called *dehiscent* fruits. Those which do not burst open are called *indehiscent*.

Dehiscent fruits

If you sit near a gorse bush or amongst a patch of campions in summer you can hear little snapping sounds as the fruits of these plants split open. Any seeds that remain inside the fruit will be tossed clear when the wind blows and shakes the dry stalks.

Dehiscent fruits may be in the form of *legumes* (or *pods*), which are formed from single ovaries; or *capsules* which, like berries, are fruits made up of a number of ovaries fused together.

▲ The broom pod twists as it splits violently open, catapulting the seeds away.

▼ The fruit of shepherd's purse, like other members of the cabbage family (Cruciferae), is made up of ovaries which pull apart when the seeds are ready for dispersal.

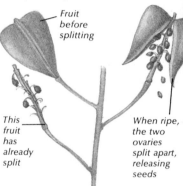

Fruit before splitting

This fruit has already split

When ripe, the two ovaries split apart, releasing seeds

▼ Campion capsules, when ripe and dry, split open at the top to release the seeds.

▼ The poppy capsule forms holes at the top when ripe, like a pepperpot.

Seeds are shaken out through holes (pores) when wind blows

Teeth: you can tell how many ovaries make up the capsule by counting the teeth

Remains of calyx (sepals)

▼ Cranesbill in fruit. The styles are fused together before the fruit is fully ripe. When it is ripe, the styles split apart rapidly and peel away upwards, flinging the single-seeded ovaries away.

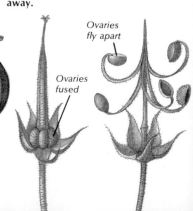

Ovaries fly apart

Ovaries fused

Indehiscent fruits

These fruits must get clear of the parent plant before the fruit wall rots and releases the seeds.

In some the seeds are so rich in food that animals will collect them and carry them off, in the same way as they do succulent fruits. This type of indehiscent fruit includes nuts such as acorns and chestnuts.

In others the ovary wall develops a rough or prickly surface, which gets caught in the fur of passing animals. Later, when the animal cleans its coat, these *burrs* are pushed off onto "new" soil.

Many indehiscent fruits have special features like wings or parachutes which enable them to be carried on the wind.

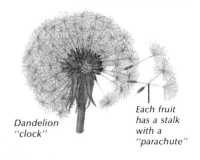

Dandelion "clock"

Each fruit has a stalk with a "parachute"

Try shaking a thistle head to see how far each parachute travels before falling to the ground

Single fruit (enlarged)

▶ The acorn nut is rich in food-stuff for animals, who collect the nuts and carry them away.

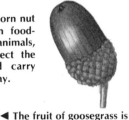

◀ The fruit of goosegrass is called a *burr*. Its rough surface with hooked hairs means it gets caught on the coats of passing animals and is carried away.

▼ The fruit wall may be expanded into a wing, as it is in ash keys below and also in maple. The wings enable the fruits to flutter away in the wind.

Winged fruit of ash

▲ Dandelion clocks and thistle down are a familiar sight. Both species belong to the daisy family (Compositae), and many plants in this family produce fruits equipped with parachutes.

In late summer notice how often the air is filled with clouds of thistle down. A few of the fruits travel enormous distances from the parent plant, but many do not get far.

Try shaking out into the wind the fruits of one thistle head to see how far each parachute travels before falling to the ground. Only those seeds which land on bare ground will be able to grow. Try and estimate the average percentage of successfully dispersed seeds in one thistle head.

23

Growth and food production

From seed to seedling (in sunflower)

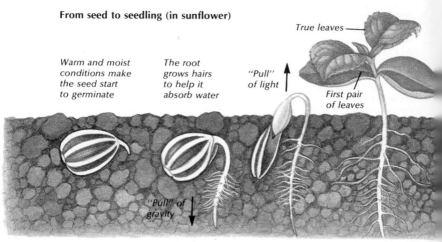

Warm and moist conditions make the seed start to germinate

The root grows hairs to help it absorb water

"Pull" of light

"Pull" of gravity

True leaves

First pair of leaves

1. At *germination*, the outer coat (testa) splits and the seedling begins to emerge.

2. Part of it becomes the root, growing downwards, guided by the force of gravity.

3. The part which becomes the shoot grows towards the light. The shoot soon grows leaves.

4. Once the leaves develop, they use energy from sunlight to make food (see below).

What makes a seed germinate?

A seed will germinate once it finds itself in a suitable habitat and once the temperature and moistness of the soil are right. The seeds of some plants require a trigger to "break their dormancy" – to stimulate them into germination. They may need to undergo something quite violent such as freezing weather or being eaten by a bird, whose digestive juices break the seed's dormancy.

Using sunlight to make food

A plant can obtain some of the nutrients it needs from the soil by absorbing them along with water through the roots. The main nutrients which can be absorbed in this way are nitrates, phosphates and potassium.

But a plant *must* also have sugars and starch which it cannot get from the soil. All green plants can use their leaves to manufacture sugars by an amazing process called *photosynthesis*. The green pigment in plants is called *chlorophyll* and this is the only substance on earth which can harness energy from *sunlight*. The energy can then be used to combine carbon dioxide and water and build energy-rich sugars and starches from them. These sugars and starches form the basis of food for all animals including humans. Oxygen, so important to animals, is given off as a by-product of photosynthesis. Without green plants, life on earth as we know it would be impossible.

Storing food

Plants often produce more sugars and starch than they need. Many can store this extra during the periods when they stop growing such as in cold times or in times of drought. The food can then be used when the plant begins to grow again and produce a new crop of leaves and/or flowers. Plants which can store food, and can therefore live for several years, are called *perennials*.

The plants which do not put by a food store, but which die within the year, after flowering and setting seed, are called *annuals*. Annuals therefore rely on their seeds germinating successfully each year in order for the species to survive. Perennials are not as dependent on this, since they will live on through the next growing season, and will have another chance to produce seeds.

Ways of storing food
Perennial plants may have one of several types of storage organs, which are "modified" stems, leaves or roots. Here are some examples.

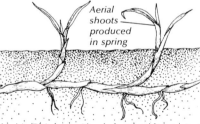

▲ *Rhizome*: Some plants such as grasses store food during winter in a horizontal underground stem called a rhizome.

Corms: Corms, such as the crocus corm, are squat underground stems which store food. Each year a new corm forms on top of the old one, which shrivels up.

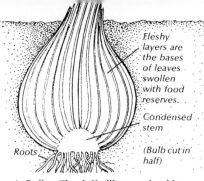

Fleshy layers are the bases of leaves swollen with food reserves.

Condensed stem

Roots

(Bulb cut in half)

▲ *Bulbs*: The daffodil stores food in a bulb, which consists of the bases of leaves swollen with food and a very short stem, and roots. Like many bulb-producing species, it can produce flowers early in the year by using its mass of stored food.

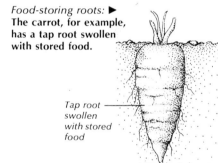

Food-storing roots: ▶
The carrot, for example, has a tap root swollen with stored food.

Tap root swollen with stored food

▼ *Tuber*: The potato plant stores food in a tuber which is in fact the swollen tip of a rhizome.

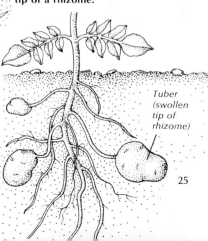

Tuber (swollen tip of rhizome)

25

Vegetative reproduction

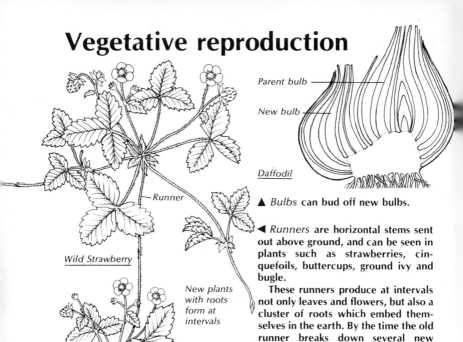

Parent bulb

New bulb

Daffodil

▲ *Bulbs* can bud off new bulbs.

Runner

Wild Strawberry

New plants with roots form at intervals

◀ *Runners* are horizontal stems sent out above ground, and can be seen in plants such as strawberries, cinquefoils, buttercups, ground ivy and bugle.

These runners produce at intervals not only leaves and flowers, but also a cluster of roots which embed themselves in the earth. By the time the old runner breaks down several new plants have become established.

If plants experience bad weather during crucial stages of their life cycle they may not be able to reproduce by means of flowers and seeds. Cold weather, high wind or rain may prevent flowers from developing, insect-pollinators from taking to the wing, or seeds from germinating.

So some plants, especially in regions with unpredictable weather, rely on other methods to reproduce. These methods usually involve a portion of the parent plant breaking off and growing into a new plant. This process is called *vegetative reproduction*.

One important but little observed method is when sections of a *rhizome* system disintegrate, leaving several separate plants. *Bulbs* bud

off new bulbs. *Tubers* separate from rhizomes and grow into new plants. Many *water plants* can reproduce vegetatively: a branch or twig broken from a willow may float downstream, lodge in a bank and sprout into a new tree. Some plants can send out *runners* (see illustration above).

Even though vegetative reproduction is very successful and often more reliable than sexual reproduction, it has two disadvantages. Firstly, only a few new plants are formed, whereas hundreds of seedlings can form as a result of sexual reproduction. Secondly, it means that all the offspring are identical to the parent, which is not always a good thing (see pages 15–18).

How flowering plants evolved

Flowering plants are the most advanced and highly evolved group of plants, as you can see from the illustrations below.

The evolutionary stages in the animal kingdom are generally better known than those of plants. Simple sea creatures were the first to evolve, followed by reptiles including dinosaurs. When the dinosaurs and other giant reptiles disap-peared, birds and mammals became more and more widespread and diverse.

The earliest plants also lived in water. About 400 million years ago new forms like mosses evolved and grew on land. Plants developed flowers at about the same time as true birds evolved and replaced the huge pterodactyls and toothed birds, about 65 million years ago.

Stages of evolution in plants

1. *Mosses* and *liverworts* have evolved from some of the earliest land plants. They can only grow when they are very damp, and, having no roots, absorb moisture all over their surface. They reproduce by spores which must fall in wet places in order to form new plants.

2. *Club mosses* and *ferns* developed roots, leaves and a system of veins to transport water from the roots to the rest of the plant. They could therefore grow taller and live in less damp places than the mosses and liverworts, but are still dependent on spores, and therefore on water, for reproduction.

3. *Conifers* produced large, strong complex seeds instead of tiny spores. The seedling needs moisture to grow but not nearly as much as spores do. Conifers could therefore grow away from damp habitats, and being strong and woody, they became very tall and dominant. But their seeds are not well protected in the cone.

4. *Flowering plants* took this system of reproduction a stage further by enclosing and so protecting the seed in an ovary.

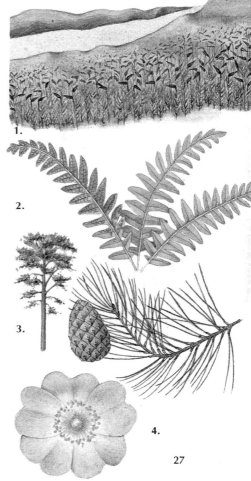

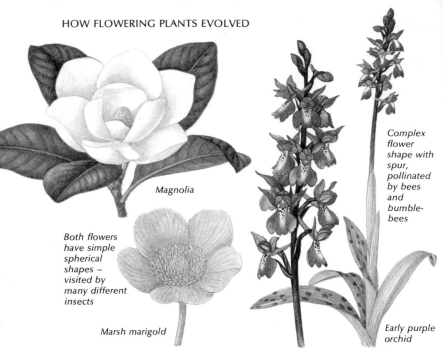

Magnolia

Complex flower shape with spur, pollinated by bees and bumble-bees

Both flowers have simple spherical shapes – visited by many different insects

Marsh marigold

Early purple orchid

▲ The magnolia and the marsh marigold are both primitively designed flowers. Notice their simple shapes and large numbers of stamens and ovaries. All kinds of insect-pollinators visit these flowers, so a large amount of pollen must be produced.

The evolution of the flower

One of the most primitively designed flowers still living today is the magnolia. In Britain one of our most primitive native flowers is the marsh marigold.

Evolution did not stop once the flower was produced. The flower produced more and more efficient methods of carrying out pollination, and the designs of the flowers became adapted to suit different pollinators, leading to the wonderful range of flowers we see today.

▲ One of the most advanced and highly evolved families of flowers in the world is the orchids. Orchids, like many other advanced flowers, single out certain insects to carry out pollination. They do this so efficiently that they need only one stamen. See also pages 38–39.

Adaptation in flowering plants

Furthermore, flowering plants continued (and still continue) to adapt themselves to survive in harsher and harsher situations, by developing features that enable them to cope with difficult conditions. They are now found in every situation on earth, even in deserts.

You can see some of the ways in which flowering plants have adapted in the following two parts of this book.

FLOWER FAMILIES
How plants are grouped

As you get to know more about flowers, it will be useful to look for similarities in the shape of the flower, and the number of parts, since it is the design alone which indicates that one flower may be related to another – and thus belong to the same family, or group.

Buttercups – a primitive family

Buttercups, crowfoots and pasque flowers, even though not of the same colour, all belong to the same family – the Ranunculaceae. Members of this family tend to have round flowers with petals of even lengths, and numerous stamens and ovaries. This is a primitive design which does not single out a particular type of insect for pollination, and must therefore produce a large quantity of pollen (see page 9).

▼ **All these flowers belong to the buttercup family. They all have lots of stamens, and petals of even length, giving the whole flower a roundish shape.**

Labiate flowers – an advanced family

Common examples of the Labiate family are yellow archangel, red dead-nettle, catmint and self-heal. In each the petals are fused together to form a long narrow corolla tube which contains the nectar. This design singles out the long-tongued insects to carry out pollination.

These flowers also provide a platform for the insect to land on, and the stamens and style arch over to touch the visiting insect's back. There are several other flowers which have this advanced design, so all are grouped together into one family – the Labiatae, illustrated overleaf.

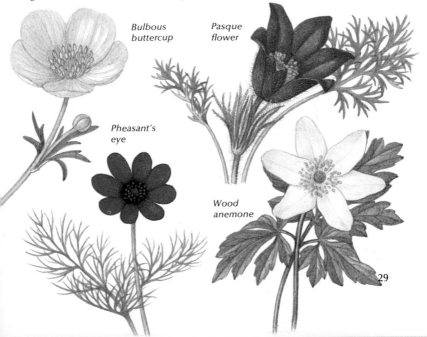

Bulbous buttercup

Pasque flower

Pheasant's eye

Wood anemone

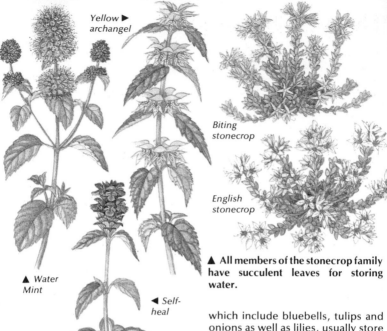

Yellow ▶ archangel

Biting stonecrop

English stonecrop

▲ Water Mint

◀ Self-heal

▲ All members of the stonecrop family have succulent leaves for storing water.

▲ Some species in the Labiate family – note the "lipped" fused petals and leaves in opposite pairs.

Other family characteristics

It is the flower of a plant which determines which family it belongs to. But members of a family often have other features in common, just because they are related.

For example, all members of the Labiate family have leaves arranged in opposite pairs, and they are also often aromatic: mints, thymes and sage are all Labiates.

The stonecrop family (Crassulaceae) has many species with succulent leaves for storing water – a useful feature in dry habitats. Members of the lily family (Liliaceae), which include bluebells, tulips and onions as well as lilies, usually store food in a bulb. This enables them to make an early start in the spring, which is very important in habitats where the summertime is not suitable for growth, so that the life cycle must be completed very early in the year.

Once you know the basic characteristics of some widespread families (see pages 31–34), you will find it much easier to identify them quickly when using a field guide in which the species are arranged in family order.

Sub-grouping in families

Most families contain so many species that they have been organized into sub-groups. These are called *genera* (*genus* is the singular form of the word). For example, *Anemone* is a genus in the buttercup family and *Mentha* (mints) is a genus in the Labiate family.

The top 20 families

When you are trying to identify an unfamiliar flower, it is fairly daunting to know that it could be any one of thousands. There are over 11,000 species in Europe, and about 1,500 of these are found in Britain.

Most identification guides show the flowers arranged in family order. So if you can recognize the family of a flower, it will save hunting through the entire book to identify it.

The "top 20"

Although there are 173 families of flowering plants represented in Europe (about 122 families in Britain), it is encouraging to know that more than three–quarters of them belong to only twenty families. So if you are able to recognize the characteristics of these top twenty, you will have found a short cut to identifying flowers.

The following notes show the main family features which will help you identify its members. The families are split into four groups. The first three – the *Dicotyledons* – contain plants with net-veined leaves (as in red campion). In the fourth group – the Mono-cotyledons – the leaf veins run *parallel* to the length of the leaf (as in tulip). The first group has small unshowy flowers, the second has petals that are *not* fused together, and the third has fused petals.

How to use the "top 20" notes

When you find an unfamiliar flower, first decide to which group it belongs (see above). All the families of flowering plants belong to one of these groups but only the top twenty families are listed on pages 32–34.

Next decide whether or not you think the plant belongs to one of these top twenty. If you think it does, turn to the pages showing the particular family in an identification book or field guide and look through for the best match. The more you use an identification book, the more you will come to recognize the characteristics which hold each family together.

If your unfamiliar plant does not seem to fit into any of the top twenty, it will be one from the other 153 families. You will find you already know something about a few of them such as the willowherbs, heathers and violets.

▼ An unfamiliar European flower could be any one of over 11,000 species. But by using the notes on pages 32–34 you will get to know the main features of the twenty most common families, and this will give you a short cut to identification.

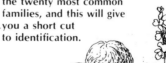

Group 1: Families with net-veined leaves and insignificant flowers (though inflorescences may be showy).

1. Willow family: Salicaceae ▼
Flowers are borne in unisexual catkins, either all male or all female on each plant. Plants are trees or shrubs. Species difficult to tell apart.

▼ 2. Dock and bistort family: Polygonaceae

3. Goosefoot family: Chenopodiaceae ▼
Both easily recognized as families, but species difficult to tell apart.

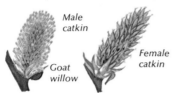
Male catkin

Goat willow

Female catkin

Common sorrel

Fat hen

Group 2: Families with net-veined leaves and unfused petals.

4. Pink family: Caryophyllaceae ▼
Petals are often cleft. Most species have five petals, some have four. Leaves in opposite pairs. Inflorescences often branched cymes.

5. Buttercup family: Ranunculaceae ▼
All flowers (except very few) have round flowers, petals of even length and numerous stamens. No epicalyx as seen in Rose family.

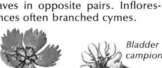
Bladder campion

Maiden pink

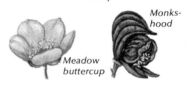
Monkshood

Meadow buttercup

6. Cabbage family: Cruciferae ▼
Flowers of all species have four widely-separated petals and usually six stamens. Many species have a raceme of small flowers. Not easily confused with Poppy family.

7. Rose family: Rosaceae ▼
All species have round flowers with petals of even lengths. Most have an epicalyx – an extra ring of sepals. Herbs, shrubs and trees.

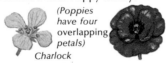
(Poppies have four overlapping petals)
Charlock

Dogrose

Epicalyx — seen from below

Cinquefoil

8. Pea family: Leguminosae ▼
Design of flowers unique – one upper standard petal, two wings and a keel. See also pages 35–36.

9. Cow parsley family: Umbelliferae ▼
Easily recognized as a family, usually with compound umbel inflorescence, but species hard to tell apart.

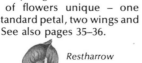
Restharrow

Hogweed

Group 3: Flowers with net-veined leaves and fused petals.

10. Primrose family: Primulaceae ▼
Round flowers with five petals of even length. Inflorescence often an umbel.

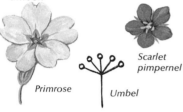

Primrose

Umbel

Scarlet pimpernel

11. Gentian family: Gentianaceae ▼
Round flowers with five petals of even length. Inflorescence usually a branched cyme. Leaves in opposite pairs.

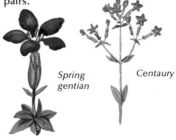

Spring gentian

Centaury

12. Forget-me-not family: Boraginaceae ▼
Round flowers with petals of even length (except for viper's bugloss), and five stamens. Often petals change colour from red (or yellow) to blue. Often inflorescence is a coiled cyme. Leaves are arranged alternately on the stem.

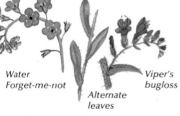

Water Forget-me-not

Alternate leaves

Viper's bugloss

13. Labiate family: Labiatae ▼
All flowers have two lips (except for bugle which has no top lip) and four stamens. Stems always square in cross-section, and leaves in opposite pairs.

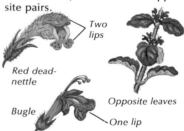

Two lips

Red dead-nettle

Bugle

Opposite leaves

One lip

14. Figwort family: Scrophulariaceae ▼
Very varied designs in flowers. For more information see page 37.

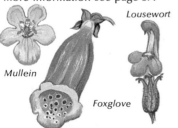

Mullein

Foxglove

Lousewort

15. Daisy family: Compositae ▼
Inflorescence a capitulum of tiny flowers (see page 6). Many species have parachuted fruits.

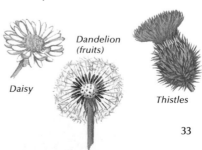

Daisy

Dandelion (fruits)

Thistles

33

Group 4: Families with parallel-veined leaves.

16. Lily family: Liliaceae ▼
The three petals and three sepals look similar. Six stamens. Many have bulbs.

Lily-of-the-valley

Chives

17. Orchid family: Orchidaceae ▼
Shapes of flowers rather varied, but always have prominent, sometimes multi-coloured, lower lips; often with spur. Only one stamen. See pages 38–39 for more information.

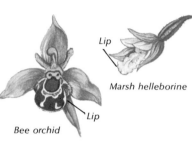

Lip

Marsh helleborine

Lip

Bee orchid

18. Rush family: Juncaceae ▼
Tiny flowers with chaffy petals. Wind-pollinated. Narrow cylindrical leaves, hollow inside, or grass-like leaves with silky hairs.

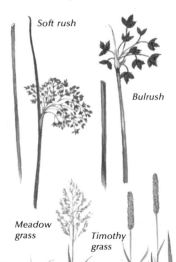

Soft rush

Bulrush

Meadow grass

Timothy grass

19. Sedge family: Cyperaceae ▼
Stems are triangular across, and the leaves are stiff. Flowers of different sexes usually in separate spikes on same stem. Wind-pollinated.

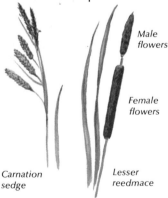

Male flowers

Female flowers

Carnation sedge

Lesser reedmace

20. ◄ Grass family: Gramineae
Tiny flowers in spikelets (see page 9) arranged in spikes or racemes.

The pea family

Surviving in poor soils

The pea family (Leguminosae) – see page 32, no. 8 – is one of the most important in the world: all its members are able to feed on nitrogen in the air. Nitrogen is one of the most essential plant nutrients. Most plants obtain it from the soil, where nitrates are dissolved in water. Soils in many places are very poor in nitrates, but the air, some of which finds its way into the soil, contains 80 per cent nitrogen. This is useless to most plants, but members of the pea family can absorb it. They do so by means of bacteria which live in lumps (nodules) in their roots. It is these bacteria which absorb the nitrogen and give it to the plant in return for sugars and a place to live. This kind of partnership, in which both organisms benefit from each other, is called *symbiosis*.

When a plant's leaves fall, and when it eventually dies, the nitrogen it accumulated is put into the soil. So pea species *improve* the nutrient level of the soil.

Nodules contain bacteria which can absorb nitrogen

▲ **Root system of a member of the pea family, showing nodules.**

The leaves

The leaves of the pea family are mostly compound – divided up into a number of smaller leaflets either in opposite pairs as in vetches or in groups of three as in laburnum and clovers. Many species have tendrils at the tip of the leaves, to help them scramble over other vegetation to reach the light.

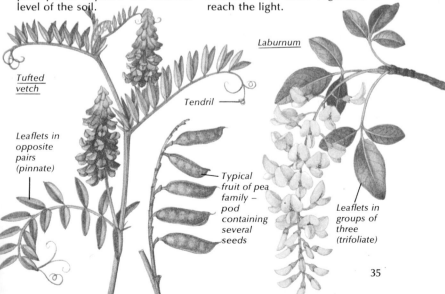

Laburnum

Tufted vetch

Tendril

Leaflets in opposite pairs (pinnate)

Typical fruit of pea family – pod containing several seeds

Leaflets in groups of three (trifoliate)

35

Flower design and pollination

At first glance a clover plant and a broom shrub do not seem to have much in common. But compare the flowers of each, shown on this page, and you will see why both are members of the pea family.

In fact all European species in this family have flowers with petals in the form of a keel, two wings and a standard. So they are all pollinated in a similar way to the broom shown below. The size of the pollinating insects varies according to the size of the flower. But, in order to obtain food – pollen or nectar – from any pea species, an insect must depress the keel, releasing the style and stamens.

Pollination in broom flowers

1. The stamens and style of a broom flower are held within the *keel*, which is flanked by two wings, with the largest petal, called a standard, upright above.
2. A bee in search of pollen (broom contains no nectar) lands on the wings of the flower. The bee's weight pushes the wings down along with the keel which bursts open immediately. The style and some of the stamens swing up and over, hitting the bee's back. So the stigma picks up pollen from other flowers which has stuck to the bee's

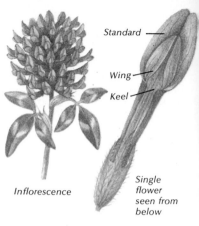

Standard
Wing
Keel
Inflorescence
Single flower seen from below

▲ If you look at a single flower in the cluster of red clover flowers, you will see its pea-like features. Like the broom below, it has a standard petal, two wings and a keel.

body, and the stamens leave their pollen on it. The bee can eat pollen left on its belly by shorter stamens, so it is enticed to carry on visiting broom flowers.

3. Once an insect has "opened" a broom flower, the keel stays down and the stamens and style cannot return to their original position. This means that the stigma cannot be pollinated if pollination fails at the first visit of a bee. But in most other members of the pea family, several visits can be made by pollinating insects.

(Broom flowers)

1.
Standard
Keel – contains stamens and style
Wing

2.
Stamens and style burst out when insect lands

3.

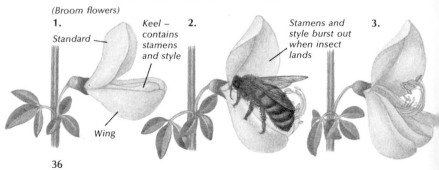

The figwort family

The figwort family (Scrophulariaceae) – see page 33, no. 14 – contains some flowers with very curious designs and some with simple shapes. Unlike most families, it is difficult to see what links them together.

But two aspects of the family can be seen quite clearly to have evolved in a very interesting way. Firstly, the designs of the flowers themselves have become more and more complicated and highly adapted: for example compare mullein to foxglove and finally to toadflax, (see pages 11 and 33).

Secondly, some of the more highly evolved plants within the family are semi-parasites. Few species of *flowering* plants are parasites. Plant parasites do not manufacture all their own sugars and starch by photosynthesis as non-parasitic plants do. Instead they sponge off other plants (their *hosts*) for some or all their nourishment. Most are particular about which host species they feed off. Grasses and members of the pea family are favourite hosts since they can flourish even on poor soils. This means that semi-parasites too can live on poor soils – but only by cheating, sponging off others.

Most of the figwort family are normal non-parasitic plants, but a number are semi-parasitic.

Some of the semi-parasites in ▶ **the figwort family have very attractive flowers, such as the eyebright and yellow rattle illustrated here, and the lousewort shown on page 47. All three feed off grasses for extra nourishment. But you can tell from their small green leaves that they *do* photosynthesize a little as well.**

No green leaves

Notice how similar the flowers are to those of eyebright below

The parasitic ▶ **broomrapes have no green leaves with which to photosynthesize. They used to be included in the figwort family, representing the final stage in the trend towards parasitism. But since broomrapes are total parasites, they have now been given a family of their own, called Orobanchaceae.**

Eyebright, a tiny flower mainly found on chalk and limestone

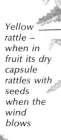

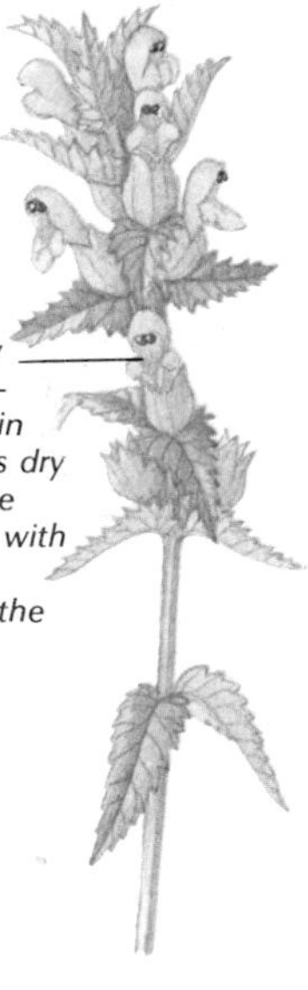

Yellow rattle – when in fruit its dry capsule rattles with seeds when the wind blows

37

The orchid family

Orchids (see page 34, no. 17) have always been one of the most popular families among flower-lovers. Many of its species are nearing extinction because of over-collection or habitat destruction. One reason why orchids are more vulnerable than other plants is that the process of seed germination is very easily disturbed.

The slow process of germination
Each orchid fruit can produce several million tiny seeds. But, unlike most plants, these seeds have no food store on which the seedling can feed during germination. The orchids are completely dependent on fungi, especially during germination (but also throughout their lives), to obtain nutrients for them.

The fungus lives protected in the seed, and later in the roots of the plant. The fungus absorbs nourishment from decaying leaves and other dead vegetation, and passes it on to the orchid. This type of partnership, in which both sides benefit, is called *symbiosis*. Despite the help from the fungi, it usually takes several years before a seed grows sufficiently mature to produce a flowering stem. So if, during this process, the soil around is disturbed, for example by ploughing, this is likely to interfere with this long maturing process.

You will find there is a great ▶ variety of curious flower designs in the orchid family. The basic features are shown in these illustrations of the common spotted orchid.

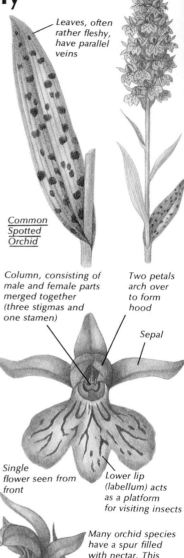

Leaves, often rather fleshy, have parallel veins

Common Spotted Orchid

Column, consisting of male and female parts merged together (three stigmas and one stamen)

Two petals arch over to form hood

Sepal

Single flower seen from front

Lower lip (labellum) acts as a platform for visiting insects

Single flower seen from side

Many orchid species have a spur filled with nectar. This singles out insect-pollinators with long probosces ("tongue

The pollen

Since orchids have very efficient and advanced methods of being pollinated, they have only one stamen. In the more primitive orchids such as the helleborines, the pollen is produced in a mass, held together by sticky threads. The more advanced species – in fact most of the other orchids – produce pollen in a few lumps called *pollinia*. The pollinia have sticky stalks which attach themselves to the pollinator's head or tongue when it visits the flower.

Orchids which mimic insects

There is a strange sub-group or genus in the orchid family, known as *Ophrys*, found mainly in southern Europe. These flowers provide no nectar to entice pollinating insects. Instead the lower lipped petal looks, feels and smells exactly like the female of certain insects. Different species of orchids of course mimic different species of insects.

When a male insect of the same species visits these flowers, he is so struck by the similarity of the lower petal to his partner that he tries to mate with it. As he does so, he picks up the pollinia on his head. When he visits another flower the pollinia are transferred to the stigmas, carrying out pollination.

So with these flowers, the visiting insects are not after food but are trying to satisfy their sexual needs.

The fly orchid mimics the female ▶ of certain wasp species. A visiting wasp is fooled into trying to mate with the lower lipped petal and, in doing so, pollinia stick to its head. The bee orchids (illustrated on page 45) are also members of the *Ophrys* genus, and mimic certain bee species.

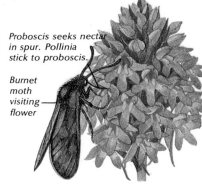

Proboscis seeks nectar in spur. Pollinia stick to proboscis.

Burnet moth visiting flower

▲ The pyramidal orchid is pollinated by butterflies and moths, whose long proboscis (or "tongues") can reach into the spur to obtain the nectar. As they do this, the pollinia stick to the proboscis and are carried to another flower.

Lower lip looks like female wasp

Male wasp tries to mate with lower lip

Pollinia

Wasp flies away with pollinia stuck to its head

FLOWER HABITATS
Why plants grow where they do

On the following pages (44–57) you will find descriptions of the main European habitats, where you will find strikingly different plant communities. These pages should help you to find out *what* plants are characteristic of these habitats, and, more importantly, *why* they grow there – especially when there are so many other habitats with more favourable conditions for plant growth.

The link between families of plants and habitats

In some habitats, several species from the same family may be found. This is often because members of that family share a special feature which equips them, above all others, to cope with the conditions there.

For example the pea family has a special characteristic which enables its members to survive in poor soil such as on heathlands (see pages 35–36 and 46–47).

The effect of the environment on plant shapes

Most habitats are shared by a large range of species, from many different families. But very often, even though they are unrelated and have very different *flowers*, their pattern of growth makes them look similar. This is because conditions in the habitat make a certain shape and pattern of growth necessary for survival there. For example, plants of high mountains tend to be low-growing – all seeming to hide from the extremes of wind and cold (see pages 56–57).

Do plants choose their particular habitat?

It is hardly ever true to say that plants grow in a particular spot because they "like" it there. What plant would choose to live at the top of a windswept mountain if it could find a spot in some fertile lowland region? Why stand in the sticky mud of an estuary and get drowned twice a day by the tides?

The answer is that by living in these grim habitats, they avoid competition from other more aggressive plants that cannot cope with such extreme conditions but that are keen fighters for space in more favourable places.

Plants compete for survival in a similar way to animals. It is easy to understand how animals competing for food will also have to compete for areas in which to hunt and graze. The strongest species will get the food first and the weaker species will have to find something else to eat, go elsewhere, or die.

In the plant world, for example, as a tree grows larger it casts shade on the plants growing below. If certain species cannot survive in the shade they must move out into the meadow and fight for a patch of soil with all the other species. If the competition is too great, they must go elsewhere or die.

If an animal or plant species can cope with a tough environment it will find a refuge away from the battleground of competition. The tough environment it finds may be in acid bogs (illustrated opposite), in the mountains, out along the coast, or deep in a shady wood.

Despite the competition, many more favourable habitats such as meadows have a wonderful variety of species, all surviving together in harmony. This is because each of them requires something different from the environment, or because their life cycles are staggered so each species flowers and fruits at a different time. In this way they do not have to compete. The struggle for survival means that every plant which survives, wherever it may be, has done so by finding a "niche".

How habitats may change

When you explore any habitat, do not imagine that it will always remain the same. Apart from the seasons, all sorts of changes take place. Bare patches of ground become carpeted with weeds, old trees eventually die allowing light to flood into a shady wood, land may suffer drought or flood, or be buried beneath an avalanche. These are all natural changes, quite apart from those brought about by people interfering with the habitat.

Some of these changes are sudden and dramatic, but most of them take place gradually. Plant communities can adjust to cope with many of these changes – some species will die out while others take the opportunity to move in.

Plant succession

If most habitats are left undisturbed, the vegetation will develop in a particular pattern. For example, if grassland is left unmown or ungrazed, it will be invaded first by scrub and eventually by woodland. Similarly, if wetland is left undisturbed, reeds will gradually help dry up the water, scrub will follow, and finally wet woodland will become established.

This natural replacement of some plants by others is called *succession*. The type of vegetation which is the last to develop, and which can last for hundreds of years, is called *climax vegetation*. The natural climax vegetation over most of Europe is forest, the type depending on local climate and soils.

▼ Plants have less competition from other species if they can adapt to an unfavourable habitat such as the bog with its soggy acid soil shown below.

Cotton-grass

Bog asphodel

Bladderwort

Pale butterwort

Cross-leaved heath

41

Wasteland weeds

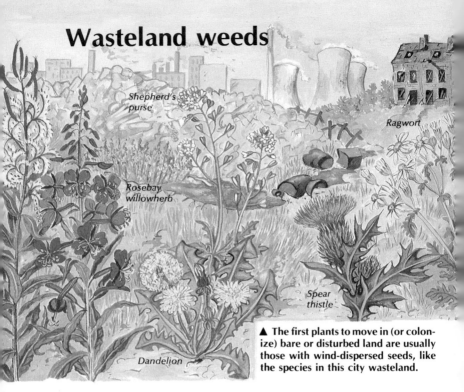

Shepherd's purse

Ragwort

Rosebay willowherb

Spear thistle

Dandelion

▲ The first plants to move in (or colonize) bare or disturbed land are usually those with wind-dispersed seeds, like the species in this city wasteland.

The land has been disturbed by people for centuries, but never more so than in the twentieth century. Areas of bare land are created all the time – on ploughed fields, embankments along highways, heavily trampled paths, gravel drives, flower beds, demolition sites and waste tips. All these places, and many others, can be called "wasteland". They all provide fresh areas for plants to colonize. Plants that move in first are known as "weeds".

Wasteland may not seem a very exciting habitat to start this section, but they are easily explored since most people pass by them every day. Wasteland can demonstrate a lot about the struggle for life amongst plants and the dispersal of seeds.

Characteristics of weeds

If you list the species found on newly-disturbed land you will find that most of them have wind-dispersed seeds. Other types of seeds may already have been present in the soil, and some may have been lying dormant for several years. But many of the plants will be those whose seeds can fly for miles on the wind – willowherbs and members of the daisy family (Compositae) such as thistles and ragworts.

The weeds seen growing most abundantly will be species which produce lots of seedlings. Often these plants produce so many flowers and seeds that they have no energy left for storing food over the winter. So many early colonizers die once they have set seed – for example the annual poppies, the biennial spear thistle and the ephemeral shepherd's purse. *Annuals* take one year to complete their life cycle, *biennials* take two years, and *ephemerals* have such a fast life cycle that they can fit in several within a season.

Survival of the early colonizers
These short-lived plants *depend* on setting seed for their survival, so most ensure that self-fertilization is possible if cross-pollination fails (see pages 15–18). Their seeds must also be sure to find bare soil on which to germinate, and there is plenty of bare soil on wasteland in its first few years.

But as more plants invade and spread on wasteland, the bare soil is taken up. Then only *perennial* plants which can store food over the winter and live for several years, will survive.

Succession of plants
So wasteland vegetation gradually changes. At first dominated by wind-dispersed annuals which produce lots of seeds, it later becomes dominated by perennials, notably grasses, which save their energy for over-wintering instead of spending it all on producing flowers and seeds. For example, the annual poppy will be squeezed out, but creeping thistles, being perennial and able to compete for space, will survive the change. This natural change is called plant succession (see page 41).

The history of weeds
Wasteland became a commonly seen habitat comparatively recently, since it occurs as a result of human activities. Yet weeds have been around a lot longer than humans. This is because wasteland sites do occur as a result of natural activity such as landslides, melting glaciers and erupting volcanoes. But bare areas produced in this way are quite rare, so many of the weeds that are now common were rare species before humans populated the earth.

▼ Cornfields, when ploughed up for sowing, provide wasteland conditions. Annuals like these poppies, charlock and mayweed may move in, giving splashes of colour amongst the wheat crop. Unfortunately, they are rarely seen, now that purer grain is sown and herbicides are used to kill "unwanted" weeds.

Chalk and limestone

The open grassland of chalk and limestone has perhaps the richest variety of flowering plants found in any habitat.

The soils

The soils that develop on chalk and limestone are known as *calcareous* soils. They are shallow and not necessarily very nutritious for plants, but they tend to be warm, being quite dry, and rich in calcium carbonate which gives them a sweet or, more correctly, *alkaline* flavour.

Most plants prefer the more alkaline soils to sour *acid* soils (see "Moors and heaths" overleaf). There are some species which can grow *only* on very calcareous soils: these are called "calcicoles".

So a rich variety of plants may grow on chalk and limestone, even in one small area. This is because no one species can become abundant enough to dominate, due to the rather unnutritious soil.

Typical plants

It is difficult to generalize about the characteristic plants, since chalk and limestone grasslands have such a wide range: they occur both in mountains and at sea level along the coast, in northern Scandinavia and on the shores of the Mediterranean. But you will always find enough "calcicoles" to indicate the soil type. Look for rockrose, salad burnet, dropwort, hoary plantain, certain orchids such as pyramidal, fragrant and bee, and grasses such as yellow oat and quaking. All these and the plants illustrated below indicate chalk and limestone areas, since they cannot grow on any other type of soil.

Grazing by animals

The rich variety of plants remains as long as the grasslands are grazed by animals. This keeps down the taller coarser plants and allows plenty of light to reach the turf. If there are

▼ The calcicoles shown below can grow on quite heavily grazed grassland. Some, like the fairy flax and squinancywort, are often too tiny to spot. But if you lie down (beware of the prickly stemless thistle!), armed with a hand lens, you will see them.

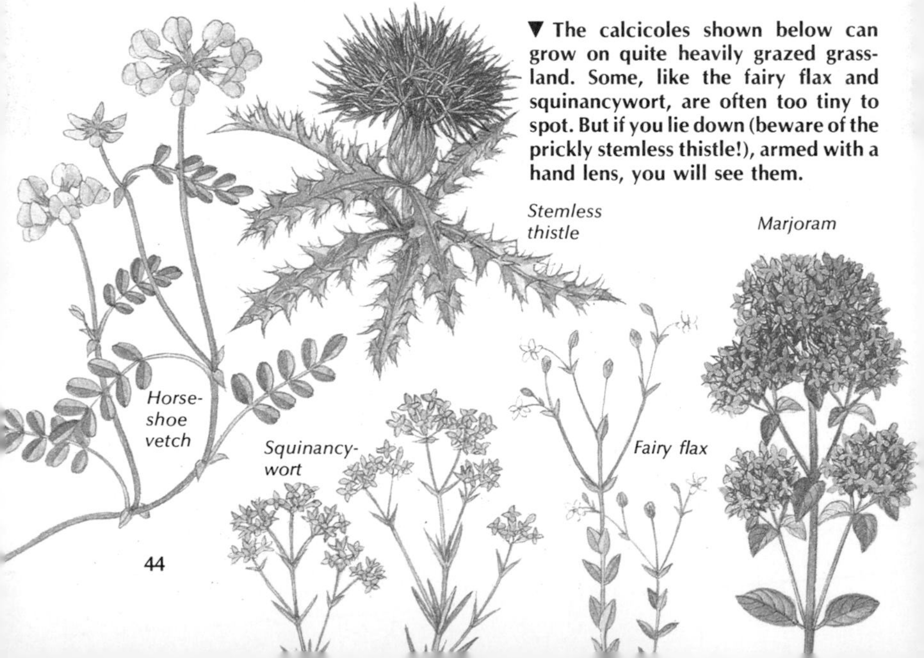

Stemless thistle

Marjoram

Horse-shoe vetch

Squinancy-wort

Fairy flax

Bee orchids
look like the
Eucera bees
which they
attract to carry
out pollination

Quaking
grass ▶

Birdsfoot trefoil

▲ Bee orchids and quaking grass are "calcicoles" which flourish in lightly grazed grassland. Many orchids, including pyramidal and fragrant, are also "calcicoles".

few grazing animals on the grassland, taller grasses such as false brome tend to overwhelm the smaller plants. Grazing will of course destroy some of the flowers, but most of the plants are perennial (see page 25) and can survive for several years without setting seed. The right balance of grazing is important: if grassland is too heavily grazed some plants may be destroyed, but if it is too light, coarse plants take over.

Trees and shrubs

If the grassland is not grazed at all, scrub soon invades and blocks out light so many species are forced out. Some bushes and trees characteristic of chalk and limestone are box and yew (both evergreen), wayfaring tree, whitebeam, dogwood, and also traveller's joy whose fluffy fruits (old man's beard) are seen in autumn.

Moors and heaths

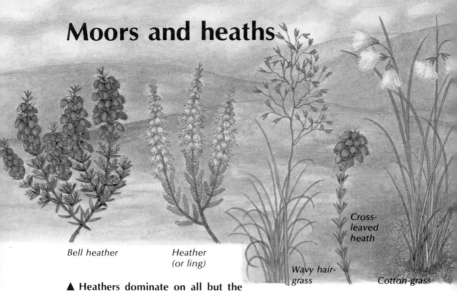

Bell heather

Heather (or ling)

Cross-leaved heath

Wavy hair-grass

Cotton-grass

▲ Heathers dominate on all but the wettest moors and heaths, where grasses and sedges tend to take over. Heather (ling) is the most dominant species, found with bell heather on very dry heathland, and sometimes with cross-leaved heath on moors and wet heaths.

Europe's vast open expanses of heathland and moorland have a very special wildness. Most of them were once forests which were felled centuries ago, and where trees have been prevented from returning. On many heaths and moors grazing by animals has stopped the natural regeneration of trees. But some moors and heaths are ancient, naturally-formed landscapes: this is especially true of those on mountains above the treeline, and in windswept coastal districts where trees cannot grow.

The rolling expanses of heather, turning purple and mauve when it flowers in late summer, give the moors and heaths their character.

The difference between moors and heaths

You may have wondered what distinguishes a moor from a heath, since both have similar vegetation. The broad definition is that moorlands occur in upland areas on damp, acid, peaty soils, while heathlands occur in lowland areas on dry, acid, sandy soils. So their similarity is due to their *acid substrate*. Substrate is a useful word which can mean solid rock, pure sand and raw compost as well as other soils. *Bogs* also have an acid substrate and boggy areas are found on both heaths and moors.

The acid soil

Whether dry and sandy or damp and peaty, this acid soil has few nutrients and is distasteful to all but a few plants. Species belonging to the heather family (Ericaceae), and some grasses and sedges, thrive on acid soil, so they tend to dominate on moors and heaths.

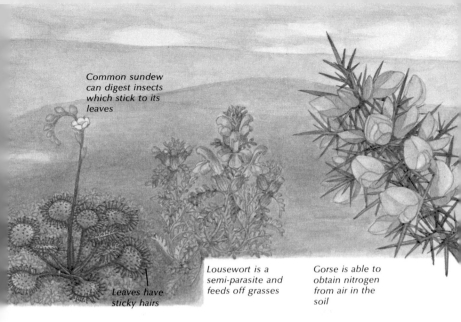

Common sundew can digest insects which stick to its leaves

Leaves have sticky hairs

Lousewort is a semi-parasite and feeds off grasses

Gorse is able to obtain nitrogen from air in the soil

The heathers that dominate

When the heather species bloom in late summer, heathland and moorland become a haze of pinks and purples. The flowers supply great quantities of nectar for insects, especially bees for whom heather is a favourite flower. Since there are few other plants in flower around, heather has the full attention of insects and a very good success rate for pollination.

Heaths and moors tend to have fairly cool and moist conditions, since they are found mainly near the sea and heather thrives in these. But it is also well-adapted to cope with any variations and extremes. Its leaves are both tiny and rolled up, which helps prevent water loss during dry periods and frost damage in winter. Also, being evergreen, it does not need to spend valuable time developing leaves each spring, and can therefore survive in cloudy upland regions where the growing season is short.

▲ The acid soils of moors and heaths are poor in nutrients, so many plants growing here get the nutrients they need from sources other than the soil.

Other plants

Moorland and heathland substrates are very poor in plant nutrients. Species belonging to the pea family (Leguminosae), such as gorse, birds -foot trefoil and vetches, can grow here since they can obtain nitrogen from air in the soil (see pages 35–36).

The semi-parasitic plants such as louseworts are found, especially on the moors (see figworts page 37). These plants can get nourishment from grasses, mainly fescue and the attractive wavy hair-grass.

On wetter ground, especially in bogs, insectivorous plants like the sundews and butterworts grow: the poor soil does not matter to them since they can supplement their diet by digesting tiny insects which get stuck to their leaves.

47

Coasts

The seaside is always fun to visit, but coastal habitats provide quite difficult conditions for plant life. Those that can grow here are fascinating, having special features in order to survive the drought, salt, and often lack of nutrients.

Types of coastline

Europe's coastline varies enormously, from high cliffs to flat coastal marshlands riddled with estuaries and creeks. The shore itself may consist of platforms of rocks or boulders, shingle, rolling sand dunes or acres of oozing mud.

All these habitats have one thing in common – they are all exposed to high winds and strong sunshine.

Drought conditions

Coastal sites do not usually have such extremes of temperature as areas inland. The strong sun and wind however dry everything out. This, together with the fact that most coastal substrates – sand, shingle, rock – cannot retain water, means that drought is a common condition on the coast. Thirst-making salt all around adds to the problems. So one of the most important features of coastal vegetation is being able to conserve water.

It is not that coastal plants *prefer* the severe conditions of drought and salt, but the few that can cope have an advantage: they have escaped from the competition between species in more favourable habitats inland, where the majority of other plants dominate.

Saltmarshes

Mud, the finest substrate of all, collects only along coasts which are quite sheltered from pounding waves. Large areas of mudflats and sand flats are often found in the mouths of estuaries and behind spits and bars (thin strips of land jutting into the sea parallel with the shore). The plant community which grows on mud and sand flats is known as saltmarsh.

At first it seems odd that a saltmarsh should have a drought problem, since it is drenched twice a day by the highest tides. But salty water is very thirst-making. What is worse, saltmarsh mud is even saltier than the sea itself, especially on sunny, windy days when pure water will evaporate from the marsh, leaving salt crystals behind. Few plants therefore can grow here and those that do have features rather similar to those found on the dry sand dunes (see pages 50–51).

One remarkable thing about saltmarsh flowers is that they are not damaged by their regular drowning

▼ Thrift is an adaptable coastal plant, growing, often in profusion, on saltmarsh, shingle, rock and on cliffs. It is also found on mountains.

Dense rosette of succulent leaves helps it to retain water

in salt water. But their *pollen* may be destroyed at high tide, so the anthers must close tightly whenever the flower is submerged.

At low tide when the marsh dries out, the flowers are visited by hoards of bees and butterflies. Notice how the flowering times of each species are spread out over the summer with little overlap. This ensures that each species has a good chance of being pollinated, by having, for most of its flowering period, the full attention of the insects. In June, thrift flowers carpet the marsh with pink. Pink turns to mauve in July and August when the sea lavender takes over. By the end of August the flowers of sea aster take their turn, continuing through into September.

Leaves are scale-like and succulent to store water

Can take root within three days if mud is not too wet

▲ Glasswort is one of the first plants to colonize the mud, helping to stabilize the shifting mud so that other salt-marsh plants can move in.

▼ A typical saltmarsh. Cord-grass is another early colonizer of the mud. Sea aster often grows in carpets over the saltmarsh, since there is little competition from other species. Sea purslane, like most saltmarsh plants, is a perennial so it will not lose its footing in the mud by dying after setting seed.

Sea aster

Cord-grass

Sea purslane

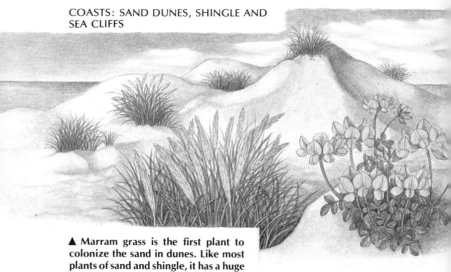

▲ Marram grass is the first plant to colonize the sand in dunes. Like most plants of sand and shingle, it has a huge root system to seek out every drop of moisture. If covered by sand, it can still grow up through it: this feature helps it to stabilize shifting sand so other plants can move in. It copes with very dry weather by rolling up its leaves to prevent too much water loss.

▲ Birdsfoot trefoil can survive in the dry acid soils of sand and shingle, which are often poor in nitrates, a nutrient which plants need. Being a member of the pea family (see pages 35–36), it can obtain nitrates in other ways.

Sand dunes and shingle beaches

More of Europe's coastline consists of sand and shingle shores than any other type. The most interesting stretches are those where the sand or shingle has built up into a series of ridges parallel with the sea – either dunes of wind-blown sand, or storm-crests of wave-tossed shingle. Here coastal plants may be found quite far inland, until they meet competition from other species.

Both sand and shingle are unable to retain water – it washes straight through, carrying any nutrients with it. The tops of the dunes and crests are therefore extremely dry, acid and poor in nutrients, but nevertheless you may find a few plants here.

But look in the dips or troughs between the ridges for the richest variety of plants. The troughs often collect water, nutrients, and shell fragments rich in lime, making them more alkaline. In dunes these troughs are called *slacks*.

If you walk over the dunes inland from the sea, you will follow the stages by which vegetation has developed, a process called succession (see page 41). The bare sand nearest the sea becomes colonized by marram grass. The farther you walk from the sea, the older the dunes are; so vegetation will have had longer to develop on the older dunes, and will be more varied. As the vegetation dies back each

COASTS: SAND DUNES, SHINGLE AND SEA CLIFFS

Sea cliffs

Few flowering plants can grow out of solid rock, but on the tops and lower ledges of cliffs, out of reach of pounding waves, a glorious variety of species may be found.

Here shallow soil forms, and conditions are easier for plants than they are on shingle, sandy and muddy shores. But the sea winds are strong and full of salt, and only some inland species can grow here. So you will find on cliffs a fascinating mixture of coastal and inland plants as well as those characteristic of mountain tops, such as thrift (see page 48). The richest variety of all grows on chalk and limestone cliffs (see pages 44–45).

▼ Sea campion, like many coastal plants, grows low on the ground to shelter from the drying wind: only the flowers are held on longish stalks to attract insect-pollinators. Its waxy leaves help prevent water loss.

English stonecrop can cling to the barest of rocky ledges. Being a succulent plant, it can store water in its leaves which helps it to survive the sun, wind and salt spray.

▲ Viper's bugloss grows in dune slacks where shell fragments have accumulated, making the sand more alkaline, and where there are more nutrients.

winter, it adds organic material to the sand. This organic matter improves conditions for plants by helping to retain water and adding nutrients to the sand.

Eventually conditions on the older dunes become so much better for plants that species that are less well-adapted to the coast can move in, and so can scrub. These gradually push the coastal plants out.

If you walk back inland from the sea over shingle ridges, the same build-up of vegetation can be observed: the older the shingle ridge, the thicker and more varied the vegetation you will find growing on it.

Sea campion

English stonecrop

Wetlands and freshwater

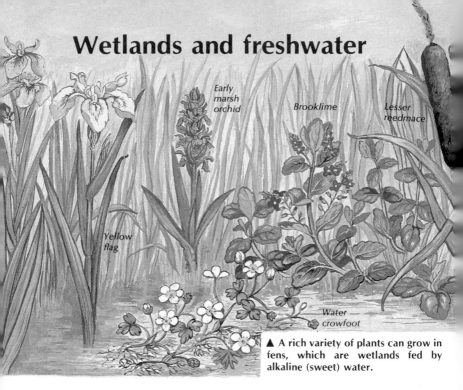

Early marsh orchid

Brooklime

Lesser reedmace

Yellow flag

Water crowfoot

▲ A rich variety of plants can grow in fens, which are wetlands fed by alkaline (sweet) water.

Watery places can harbour a wealth of colourful flowers, especially in summer. Look for these along river-banks, around lakes and ponds, in marshes, bogs and damp meadows. You will find different types of plants according to the amount of water, and to its type – acid or alkaline.

Wetlands: marshes, bogs, fens
You may have wondered what the difference is between these types of wetland. The different types of wet-land are determined by their soil and water.

Marsh is a more general term for wetland, but, unlike bogs and fens, marsh soils have very little organic material, and no peat at all. Peat is dead plant material which is only partially decayed.

Bogs are *acid* and, just as on moors and heaths (see pages 46–47), the acid conditions limit the variety of plants which can grow. On bogs, look out for cotton-grass, mosses, members of the heather family such as cross-leaved heath and cranberry and the strange insectivorous plants like the sundews and butterworts.

Fens are fed with *alkaline* water draining from chalk and limestone hills. So, like chalk and limestone grassland (see pages 44–45), a rich variety of plants can grow on fens.

All types of wetlands are threatened habitats, especially fen-land which, once drained, provides valuable agricultural land.

Wetland plants as "indicators"
When you visit any habitat, notice

how dramatically the vegetation changes wherever there is a lot of water. Wetland plants can indicate extra moisture in the soil when you are out walking. Often the strong smell of water mint leaves, crushed underfoot, is the first warning of soggy ground on an apparently dry path. A ribbon of yellow marsh marigolds may pick out the course of a tiny stream cutting through a field.

Plants of open water

Most aquatic plants hold their flowers above water for pollination, usually by insects. Notice how many water plants have submerged leaves which look different from those above water. In fact the underwater leaves often look more like green roots. This is because they are very finely divided in order to flow freely with the moving water, and yet still have a good surface area for carrying out photosynthesis.

Wetland succession

The pond illustrated below will not naturally remain the same size or depth over the years. Open water will give way to reeds which in turn give way to scrub, in the following stages.

1. Every autumn dead vegetation builds up at the bottom of the pond. There is so little air here that the vegetation does not decompose properly, and forms layers of peat.

2. The water gradually becomes shallower and the fringe of *reeds* spreads in towards the centre of the pond. This forces plants of open water into yet deeper water to avoid being overshadowed by reeds.

3. Wetland scrub, called *carr*, consisting of alders, willows and buckthorns, moves into the reed bed, shading out the reeds.

This is another example of plant succession, which eventually leads to the pond drying out and the wetland scrub taking over.

3. Carr (wetland scrub)

2. Reed bed

1. Open water

53

Woodlands

When you visit an area, the type of trees growing there can tell you a lot about local conditions. For instance, most willows grow only on damp soils, while birch prefers well-drained, usually sandy soils. Ash and beech favour nutrient-rich alkaline ground, while many pines grow better in acid soil with few nutrients.

Conifers are usually hardier than broadleaved trees, and better able to withstand cold and drought. Conifers are therefore found further north and at higher altitudes, and also on very dry coastal districts.

Looking for flowers in woods

Deciduous woods are the most rewarding for plant hunters. Few plants grow in evergreen woods, especially coniferous ones which produce a deep acid litter of needles in which hardly any plants can grow, even if light could penetrate the wood.

But keep a look-out for flowers such as bugle and trailing St John's wort in the open glades and edges of walks and rides in all woods. Natural woods, as opposed to plantations, include trees of different ages and have open spaces where old trees have died and fallen. So natural woods contain the greatest variety of flowers.

▲ Primroses, being perennials, use the food stored in their roots to produce leaves early in the year (see page 25). They are therefore able to flower in spring before the woodland floor becomes shaded by the leaf canopy above.

Deciduous woods in spring

Primroses, violets and bluebells are the most well-known woodland flowers. They all flower in spring. This is not just a coincidence: most woodland plants time their life cycle so they flower before the canopy of leaves above shades the woodland floor. So, by avoiding competition from the hundreds of plants which need summer sunshine and must fight for space in the open, woodland flowers find a refuge.

In fact they have so little competition from other species that they grow in huge numbers. Primroses, bluebells and wood anemones often grow in carpets on the more acid soils; ramsons and lily-of-the-valley often carpet the more alkaline woodland soils.

▼ This tiny spring-flowering plant, moschatel, is often overlooked in woods. It is also called "town hall clock" because it has four clock-like faces.

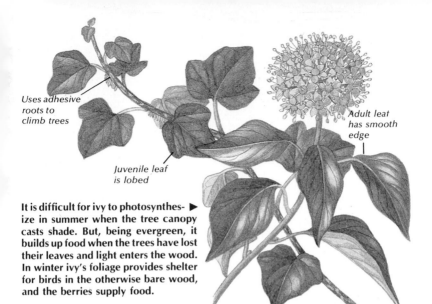

Uses adhesive
roots to
climb trees

Adult leaf
has smooth
edge

Juvenile leaf
is lobed

It is difficult for ivy to photosynthes- ▶
ize in summer when the tree canopy
casts shade. But, being evergreen, it
builds up food when the trees have lost
their leaves and light enters the wood.
In winter ivy's foliage provides shelter
for birds in the otherwise bare wood,
and the berries supply food.

Plants that can live in shade

During summer, although the full
leaf canopy casts shade, a small
amount of light can filter through, so
you will usually find some plants
growing below. Some species have
features which enable them to live in
shady places.

Ivy and honeysuckle are climbers
and can reach light by climbing
trees. Their flowers are borne only
on stems which have found their
way into some light.

Look at the leaves of plants which
can grow in shade as well as sun –
bramble, ground ivy or stinging nettle: you may find the leaves in the
shade are larger than those in the
sun, so as to catch more light.

A few species use another source
of energy instead of light to produce
food, in the same way that fungi do.
These are either saprophytic (feeding on decaying matter), or parasitic
(feeding on living plants or animals).
Yellow bird's-nest, for example, is a
saprophyte found in beech and pine
woods.

Tree flowers

All trees except conifers bear
flowers. Catkins are usually produced in late winter or early spring,
before the foliage develops. The
leaves would prevent pollen from
moving freely in the wind (see pages
13–14). Blossoms usually flower later
in the year, when the highest numbers of pollinating insects are about.

▼ Notice how similar these two woodland flowers look, though wild strawberry is a herb and hawthorn is a tree.
Both species belong to the Rose family
(see page 32).

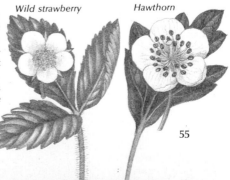

Wild strawberry   Hawthorn

Mountains

Look for these different zones as you climb a mountain, but bear in mind that most of the trees may have been cleared. ▶

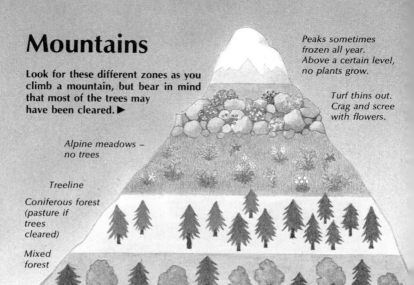

Peaks sometimes frozen all year. Above a certain level, no plants grow.

Turf thins out. Crag and scree with flowers.

Alpine meadows – no trees

Treeline

Coniferous forest (pasture if trees cleared)

Mixed forest

The mountains, with their fresh air and glorious scenery, are very enjoyable places in which to look for flowers.

As in most habitats, the variety of plants will depend on the soil, which in turn depends on the rock below and on the climate. See "Chalk and limestone" and "Heaths and moors" (pages 44–47) for information about the difference between alkaline and acid soils and rocks. In the limestone mountains of southern Europe, with its sunnier climate, the plants are richer in variety than in the cool, wet granite hills of northern Scotland.

The lower pastures and forests

As you wend your way uphill you may pass through many different habitats. The illustration shows broadly the types of vegetation which occur naturally at different altitudes. Both coniferous and broadleaved woodland may be found lower down, but further up only conifers can survive. But in both these zones the trees may have been cleared, leaving pastures.

If the lower slopes are not wooded, try to decide why not. Is it because the forest has been cleared? Is the vegetation being grazed too heavily, preventing trees and shrubs from growing up? Has there been an avalanche in the last century? Or is the climate so wet and cool that acid blanket bog (see "Wetlands" pages 52–53) has developed, as it has in large areas of Scotland. Very few plants can grow on these acid blanket bogs.

The level at which the conifer trees thin out and stop growing is called the treeline. It is interesting to compare the different bands of vegetation on opposite sides of a valley. On south-facing slopes, which are generally warmer and sunnier for longer periods of the year, the treeline is usually higher up than on the north-facing slopes, where the snow lies for longer.

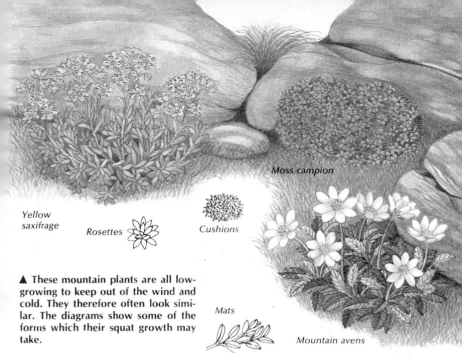

Yellow saxifrage

Rosettes

Cushions

Moss campion

Mats

Mountain avens

▲ These mountain plants are all low-growing to keep out of the wind and cold. They therefore often look similar. The diagrams show some of the forms which their squat growth may take.

Higher up the mountains – the alpine meadows

As you walk out above the lush meadows and forest and above the treeline, the turf gets shorter. The flowers are often large compared with the rest of the plant. Look out for flowers belonging to the gentian, primrose and buttercup families. These are often seen bursting into flower before the snow around them has completely melted. The flowers must get off to an early start with such a short growing season ahead of them before the snow returns.

The mountain peaks

The turf begins to thin out further up. More low-growing plants festoon the crags and scree, but sometimes you will need to hunt among the boulders to see them. These plants must grow low so as to keep out the wind and avoid damage by

frost and wind; another reason for this is that they have only a short summer season in which to grow.

Though their squat growth makes all the plants look rather similar, there is a great variety of species from several different families, and their flowers vary enormously in glorious colours and designs. This is because many mountain plants are insect-pollinated. But at very high altitudes, especially in the mountains of northern Europe, weather conditions may sometimes be too severe for insects to survive. So the further north you are, the more you find that mountain plants are pollinated by wind rather than by insects. Those that *are* insect-pollinated have devices to ensure that self-pollination takes place in case cross-pollination fails (see page 18). Most of them rely heavily on vegetative reproduction (see page 26).

The field botanist

You can learn something about the natural world from books, but it is much more exciting and informative to build on this knowledge by exploring for yourself.

All habitats and their wild plants and animals are threatened with extinction because of human activities. In order to try and conserve them, we should understand as much about them as possible. This book is only an introduction to the flowering plants, but it may have suggested ways of looking at them in the wild, and of understanding how and why they grow where they do.

How to use a hand lens: Hold the lens steady and close to your eye. Bring the flower into focus by moving closer.

Understanding more about plants

Wherever you go, try not to take the plants around you for granted. Ask yourself questions: what species are these? How did they get here? Why these species and not others? How do they survive and how long will they stay? What creatures live amongst them? The answers will not always be obvious, but you will begin to learn to interpret what you see.

Looking at flowers

Never pick flowers – many species have become extinct through over-picking. When identifying, take the book to the flower not the flower to the book (see page 62 for suggested field guides). Try to carry a hand lens to observe tiny features. *Naming* the species should not be an end in itself – use it as a key to discover more information. Most books indicate a plant's usual habitats. After a while you will be able to use flowering plants as indicators of local conditions. You can also use the hand lens to find out how a flower is pollinated. Is the flower dichogamous (see page 16)? What kind of pollinator is it designed to attract? You may well be able to observe the pollinating insects at work.

▼ Two sketches of the same heathland area both made in August: the one on the left was made two years after a fire, the one on the right three years after that. Notice the changes. You can record them in the way suggested opposite.

58

Heathland : vegetation each August

	76	77	78	79	80	81	82
Bare ground	100%	50%	10%				
Rosebay Willowherb		10%					
Gorse			5%	10%	20%	30%	30%
Lichens and Mosses			5%	30%	15%	10%	10%
Bracken			20%	30%	20%	20%	10%
Grasses			10%	20%	50%	30%	20%
Heather			5%	15%	30%	40%	60%

Roadside verge at crossroads: species in flower (✓ = flowering)

	March 1 15	April 1 15	May 1 15	June 1 15	July 1 15	Aug 1 15
Primrose	✓✓	✓✓				
Bluebell		✓✓	✓✓			
Dandelion			✓	✓✓✓	✓	
Cow Parsley			✓	✓✓		
Rough chervil				✓✓	✓✓	✓
Self heal					✓	✓✓
Foxglove					✓	✓✓

▲ Recording yearly changes: In the dry summer of 1976 fire destroyed vast areas of this piece of heathland. Nothing survived immediately after the fire, but over the following years heathland vegetation slowly grew back. The record above shows in what order and in what quantities each species returned. Each August the same area was visited and the *percentage* of ground covered by each species was estimated and recorded. Each new species as it occurred was added to the bottom of the list.

Recording changes in habitats

If you are able to make several visits to a habitat, however small, you can learn a lot by recording changes which take place – two methods are illustrated above. If your area is interfered with by humans in any way, make a note of what happened (for example heathland burned, a hedge cut, a pasture ploughed) and carry on recording how the plants respond.

▲ Recording short-term changes: A similar method can be used to record weekly or monthly events. Try looking at the flowering sequence along a roadside verge. This record shows both how long each species was in flower and the variety in flower at the same time.

Notice how the flowering periods of closely-related species, such as those in the cow parsley family, hardly ever overlap. This makes sure that each species has good chance of being pollinated.

Looking at flowers on holiday

Before you go on holiday, try and find out what sort of plants you might expect to find in the place you will be visiting. What is the local geology like? Is the area renowned for any special or rare plants? If the habitats in your holiday area are unfamiliar, think what their important features might be and how the plants might be adapted to cope with conditions.

FURTHER INFORMATION
Famous botanical sites

Wherever you are in Britain, you will be able to find at least a few wild flowers, and there are hundreds of places where a wide selection can be seen. Some sites, because of their position and geology, have an exceptional variety and a few of these are listed below.

Most of them are nature reserves and permits may be required to visit them. Visitors should stay on rights of way and not pick, uproot or otherwise disturb the plants; make sure your visit does not spoil the site for other people.

Further details of interesting sites in Britain are given in books such as "Finding Wild Flowers" by R. S. R. Fitter, published by Collins, and in the Nature Guides, published by Usborne.

CHALK AND LIMESTONE
CHALK:
North and **South Downs** of south-east England, particularly Kent and Sussex.
LIMESTONE:
Cotswolds, Gloucestershire.
Derbyshire Dales.
Wye Valley, Gloucestershire and Herefordshire.
Avon Gorge, Avon.
Upper Teesdale, Durham.
Mendip Hills in Somerset, for example **Cheddar Gorge** and **Brean Down**.
Ormes Head, Gwynedd, north Wales.
Gower Peninsula, West Glamorgan, south Wales.
Durness, Highland Region, Scotland.
Limestone "pavements" (bare fissured rock) are found in **Cumbria**,

the **Craven** district of the Pennines in Yorkshire, and in **The Burren**, Co. Clare, Ireland.

LOWLAND HEATHLAND
The **Breckland** of Norfolk and Suffolk (around Thetford) – heathland and chalk grassland are mixed here.
New Forest, Hampshire.
Dorset heaths, for example Studland and Wareham.
Lizard Peninsula, Cornwall (on serpentine rock).
Coastal heaths of **Suffolk**.

COASTAL SITES
Lizard Peninsula, Cornwall (also listed under "Lowland heathland".
Ormes Head, Gwynedd, north Wales, and the **Gower Peninsula**, West Glamorgan, south Wales, both also listed under "Limestone".
Isles of Scilly
SAND DUNES:
Braunton Burrows, Devon.
Isle of Anglesey, Gwynedd, north Wales.
Southport to **Formby**, Lancashire.
The **Lincolnshire** coast.
North Norfolk coast (dunes, shingle and saltmarsh occurs from **Hunstanton** to **Sheringham**).
Machair on the sandy west coasts of the **Western Isles**, Scotland.
SALTMARSHES:
Essex, south **Suffolk**, the **Thames Estuary** (Kent and Essex), and the **Wash** (Lincolnshire/Norfolk).
SHINGLE:
North Norfolk (see under "Sand dunes" above).
Chesil beach, Dorset.
Dungeness, Kent.

WETLANDS:
Canals, meres and bogs of **Shrop-** and **Cheshire**.
The **Norfolk Broads**, for example **Ranworth Broad**. Fens and marshes of East Anglia, for example **Wicken Fen**, Cambridgeshire.
Sedgemoor, Somerset.

WOODLANDS
Highlands of **Kerry** and **Cork**, Ireland, where Lusitanian species occur (ie. species found chiefly in Spain and Portugal).
Derbyshire ashwoods.
Oak and mixed woods of the **Weald**, especially in Kent and Sussex.
Epping Forest, Essex.
Forest of Dean, Gloucestershire.

MOUNTAINS
Ben Lawers, Highland Region, Scotland: this is the most important site in Britain for arctic-alpine plants.
Cairngorms, Highland and Grampian Regions, Scotland.
Snowdonia, north Wales.
Lake District, Cumbria.
Donegal, Ireland, where arctic-alpine plants occur near sea level.

▼ **Though Britain has a relatively limited number of plant species, some of the sites listed above are of international interest. Every country of course has its specialities, and very rich sites can be found in other parts of Europe. Shown below is an alpine meadow in the Pyrenees, Andorra.**

Useful addresses

One of the best ways of learning more about the countryside is to go out with others. Some societies arrange field days; the leader may be a specialist or an all-round naturalist.

Wild Flower Society, 68 Outwoods Road, Loughborough, Leicestershire LE11 3LY. Members keep a diary to record where and when species are seen in flower. These diaries can be submitted in a competition to find out who saw most species in flower each year.
Botanical Society of the British Isles, c/o Dept. of Botany, British Museum (Natural History), Cromwell Road, London SW7 5BD. A more learned society which encourages junior members and amateurs and anyone involved in research (such as the records suggested on pages 58–59).
County Naturalists' Trust. You can get the address of your local Trust from the Royal Society for Nature Conservation, 22 The Green, Nettleham, Lincoln LN2 2NR. They will also give you information about the **WATCH** club – the junior branch of the Nature Conservation Trusts. WATCH has its own magazine, projects and local groups.
County or Local Natural History Societies. You can get the address of your local Society from CoEnCo, Zoological Gardens, Regents Park, London NW1. They plan programmes of talks and outings each year.
The Field Studies Council, Information Office, Preston Montford, Montford Bridge, Shrewsbury SY4 1HW. Runs outdoors courses in different aspects of natural history including wild flowers, held at its nine residential centres in Britain.
British Trust for Conservation Volunteers, 36 St Mary's Street, Wallingford, Oxon OX10 0EU, arrange task forces throughout Britain. You will learn most about the hard labour involved in tasks such as clearing scrub, but you will also learn about the habitat you are working on.

Books

The notes on pages 31–34 offer an introduction to the identification of flowers, but you will need a more comprehensive field guide. Here are some suggestions.

Flowers of Britain and Northern Europe by Fitter, Fitter and Blamey (Collins). Illustrations and short descriptions of each species.
The Excursion Flora of the British Isles by Clapham, Tutin and Warburg (Oxford University Press). No illustrations but detailed descriptions, with keys, of all species and their habitats.
These first two books work very well if used together.
Atlas of the Flowers of Britain and Northern Europe by Fitter (Collins) has maps showing where you could expect to find each species.
Usborne Guide to Wild Flowers by Barry Tebb (Usborne). Flowers arranged by colour.
The **New Naturalist** series, published by Collins, has some interesting titles such as **Flowers of Chalk and Limestone** and **Flowers of the Coast**. In these you will find full lists of the characteristic species of the different habitats. Also look out for books on the wild flowers or general natural history of your local area. These can give you useful background information about the area.

Index of Latin names

Here is a list of the Latin names of flowers mentioned and illustrated in the book. It is useful to know these, since the Latin name of a species is standard throughout the world, whereas the common names of flowers can vary even from region to region in Britain. For example, meadow sage is also known as meadow clary, and thrift as sea pink.

hazel, *Corylus avellana*
heath, cross-leaved, *Erica tetralix*
heather, *Calluna vulgaris*
   bell, *Erica cinerea*
helleborine, marsh, *Epipactis palustris*
hemlock, *Conium maculatum*
hogweed, *Heracleum sphondylium*
honeysuckle, *Lonicera periclymenum*
ivy, *Hedera helix*
   ground, *Glechoma hederacea*
lavender, sea, *Limonium vulgare*
lily-of-the-valley, *Convallaria majalis*
ling, *Calluna vulgaris*
loosestrife, purple, *Lythrum salicaria*
lousewort, *Pedicularis*
lupin, *Lupinus*
magnolia, *Magnolia*
marigold, marsh, *Caltha palustris*
marjoram, *Origanum vulgare*
mayweed, scentless, *Tripleurospermum inodorum*
meadow rue, *Thalictrum flavum*
mint, water, *Mentha aquatica*
monkshood, *Aconitum*
moschatel, *Adoxa moschatellina*
mullein, *Verbascum*
nettle, stinging, *Urtica dioica*
old man's beard, *Clematis vitalba*
orchid, bee, *Ophrys apifera*
   common spotted, *Dactylorhiza fuchsii*
   early marsh, *Dactylorhiza incarnata*
   early purple, *Orchis mascula*
   fly, *Ophrys insectifera*
   fragrant, *Gymnadenia conopsea*
   pyramidal, *Anacamptis pyramidalis*
pansy, wild, *Viola tricolor*
pasque flower, *Pulsatilla vulgaris*
pheasant's eye, *Adonis*
pimpernel, scarlet, *Anagallis arvensis*
pink, maiden, *Dianthus deltoides*
plantain, hoary, *Plantago media*
poppy, common, *Papaver rhoeas*
primrose, *Primula vulgaris*
purslane, sea, *Halimione portulacoides*

ragwort, *Senecio*
ramsons, *Allium ursinum*
rattle, yellow, *Rhinanthus minor*
reed, *Phragmites australis*
reedmace, lesser, *Typha angustifolia*
restharrow, *Ononis repens*
rose, dog, *Rosa canina*
rush, bulrush, *Schoenoplectus lacustris*
   soft rush, *Juncus effusus*
sage, meadow, *Salvia pratensis*
St John's wort, *Hypericum*
saxifrage, yellow, *Saxifraga aizoides*
sedge, carnation, *Carex panicea*
self-heal, *Prunella vulgaris*
shepherd's purse, *Capsella bursa-pastoris*
snapdragon, *Antirrhinum*
sorrel, common, *Rumex acetosa*
squinancywort, *Asperula cynanchica*
stonecrop, biting, *Sedum acre*
   English, *Sedum anglicum*
strawberry, wild, *Fragaria vesca*
sundew, common, *Drosera rotundifolia*
sunflower, *Helianthus*
sycamore, *Acer pseudoplatanus*
teasel, *Dipsacus fullonum*
thistle, creeping, *Cirsium arvense*
   spear, *Cirsium vulgare*
   stemless, *Cirsium acaule*
thrift, *Armeria maritima*
thyme, *Thymus*
toadflax, *Linaria vulgaris*
traveller's joy, *Clematis vitalba*
trefoil, bird's foot, *Lotus corniculatus*
vetch, horseshoe, *Hippocrepis comosa*
   tufted, *Vicia cracca*
violet, *Viola*
wayfaring tree, *Viburnum lantana*
whitebeam, *Sorbus aria*
willow, crack, *Salix fragilis*
   goat, *Salix caprea*
willowherb, rosebay, *Chamerion angustifolium*
yellow archangel, *Lamiastrum galeobdolon*
yew, *Taxus baccata*

WATCHING
BIRDS

INTRODUCTION

Birdwatching is one of today's fastest growing pursuits. Literally millions of Europeans own a bird identification book and in Britain at least half a million people belong to the groups and societies that monitor the fortunes of birds and protect the increasingly precious habitats that they share with us.

This section of the book is about getting to know birds and studying their ways of life. The world of birds is an exciting and fascinating one, full of endless questions and sometimes surprising answers.

For a start, where should you look to find birds? The pages on reading habitat give a lot of clues on how to look at a landscape and pick out the areas that are rich in birds. Once you know how to find these areas you will come across all sorts of bird behaviour that will set you thinking.

You may find a bird roost and want to start counting and identifying the birds that come in. Once you start looking at birds questions will spring to mind. Do blue tits, for instance, feed on the ground and right up a tree as far as the topmost branches

in your area? Are great tits feeding in the same places? How do gales affect flying birds? Which species migrate through your area and in which direction are they going? You may have mallard and tufted ducks on a nearby lake. How are they both able to feed on the same area of water? Why isn't there competition between them? And what are skylarks doing on your local football pitch? The following chapters suggest ways of finding answers to these and many other questions.

This section is full of practical ideas to start you off on the study of birds. There's a lot of information on how to watch birds and the techniques you can use to study bird behaviour and to survey bird movements and populations.

The studies suggested here do to some extent follow on, one from the other, but you can, of course, pick those you are most interested in.

If you come across a term you do not understand, look it up in the index. It may have been explained earlier, usually on the first page listed in the index.

A careful observer watches a wheatear feeding its young, without disturbing the birds.

STARTING OFF
Identifying birds

In the next few pages I deal with the basic principles of identification, but the real art is, as with most skills, largely a matter of practice – and that is up to you.

There are about 8,500 species of birds in the world and Europe has 725 of these, grouped in families. (The relationship between families and species is explained more fully on page 80).

The aim of identification is to recognize and name an individual species. For practical purposes you need to narrow a bird down to its family group. This will leave you to select between a limited number of species to make the final identification.

The first step in this process of elimination is to get to know the different families. An understanding of the relationships between them will help.

Scientists have arranged the families (and the species within them) in a "systematic order", placing related families close together. There are several accepted systematic orders, each slightly different, but basically they all start with the families that evolved first and end with the most recently evolved.

Most field guides (identification

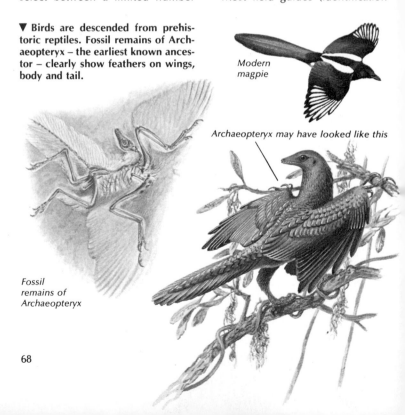

▼ Birds are descended from prehistoric reptiles. Fossil remains of Archaeopteryx – the earliest known ancestor – clearly show feathers on wings, body and tail.

Modern magpie

Archaeopteryx may have looked like this

Fossil remains of Archaeopteryx

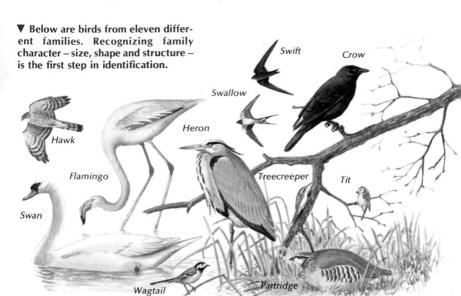

▼ Below are birds from eleven different families. Recognizing family character – size, shape and structure – is the first step in identification.

Swift

Crow

Swallow

Heron

Hawk

Treecreeper

Tit

Flamingo

Swan

Wagtail

Partridge

books) follow one of the systematic orders. So, study the illustrations and descriptions in a field guide (more information on field guides on pages 106 and 127) and you will start to become familiar with the characteristics of each family.

What to look for in the field
There are four main types of difference that will enable you to identify

a bird. Firstly *general character* or *"jizz"* (the bird's personality, structure and actions), secondly *plumage* (the coloured patterns or "feather map"), thirdly *voice* (the calls and song) and fourthly *behaviour* (both the individual and social acts of the bird).

Make notes on all these things and you will have a good description from which to identify the bird.

▼ Plumage patterns within a family are usually quite different – as with these three tits.

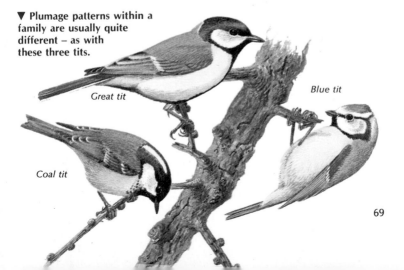

Great tit

Blue tit

Coal tit

69

Seasonal changes in bird population

An important aid to bird identification is a knowledge of the annual cycle of bird events. Each season brings a change in dominant weather, affecting the safe cover and food available and, consequently, the bird population. Knowing what to expect is therefore important.

Resident birds move to different areas during the year, migrants arrive and leave, and vagrants can turn up at any time. So be ready for birds that have flown across the Atlantic from America and others that have struggled all the way from Siberia.

All in all, bird identification is a big subject, and a disciplined approach is crucial to solving its many fascinating problems. You will find it helpful to read carefully the later sections in this book, such as "Learning key species" (page 80).

▼ Birds on the edge of a wood in summer (left) and winter (right), showing how the bird population in a common habitat changes with the seasons.

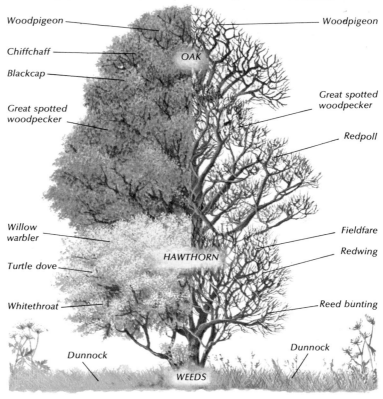

Woodpigeon — Woodpigeon
Chiffchaff
Blackcap
OAK
Great spotted woodpecker
Great spotted woodpecker
Redpoll
Willow warbler
Turtle dove
HAWTHORN
Fieldfare
Redwing
Whitethroat
Reed bunting
Dunnock
Dunnock
WEEDS

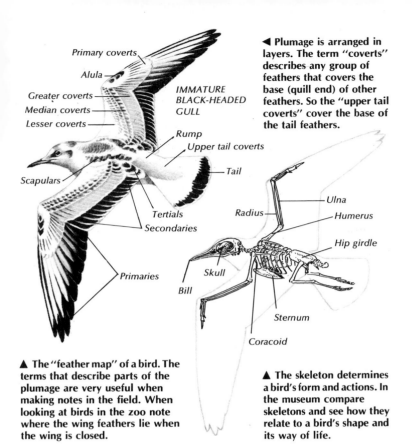

Primary coverts

Alula

Greater coverts

Median coverts

Lesser coverts

IMMATURE
BLACK-HEADED
GULL

Rump

Upper tail coverts

Tail

Scapulars

Tertials

Secondaries

Radius

Ulna

Humerus

Hip girdle

Primaries

Skull

Bill

Sternum

Coracoid

◀ Plumage is arranged in layers. The term "coverts" describes any group of feathers that covers the base (quill end) of other feathers. So the "upper tail coverts" cover the base of the tail feathers.

▲ The "feather map" of a bird. The terms that describe parts of the plumage are very useful when making notes in the field. When looking at birds in the zoo note where the wing feathers lie when the wing is closed.

▲ The skeleton determines a bird's form and actions. In the museum compare skeletons and see how they relate to a bird's shape and its way of life.

Taking a close look at birds

Dashing out with a field guide open in one hand and binoculars clutched in the other is the sure way to make immediate mistakes in bird identification.

A less frustrating way to start would be to visit two good places to see birds: your local museum and the nearest zoo. There you can have a good look at the birds with an opportunity of close study for a long period that is hard to get in the field. Try to visit them with an experienced birdwatcher and learn as much as you can from the museum's stuffed specimens or the zoo's collection of captive birds.

Remember to look at skeletal structure (in the museum), and plumage contours or the overlay of feathers (at the zoo), for together these, with the bird's muscles, determine its visible form and actions. Try to define what you see and so develop the invaluable habit of constantly cross-referring between the written word and the living bird. Start by taking notes on the birds you observe and compare your notes later with the descriptions in your field guide.

Approaching birds

To get close to birds – and have the wonderful thrill of a live, wild, flying animal at ease before you – you have to accept the role of hunter and practise fieldcraft, until its various rules are second nature to you.

The more obvious rules in stalking are quietness and careful move-ment, unobtrusiveness (using every scrap of cover) and camouflage (avoid gaudy anoraks), and steady concentration on the bird(s) ahead. Less obvious but equally important factors are the angle of maximum light (preferably kept to one side or behind you), the choice of sheltered and comfortable observation points (watering eyes see only blurs!) and patience. A sudden charge will have only one result – the fast retreating rear end of an escaping bird.

The alternative to stalking is to settle yourself down in a bird-rich habitat and let them come to or past you. These days bird reserves are surrounded by hides (wooden shel-ters with observation slits) and a watch from one can be spellbinding, so close do the birds approach. Hides are, however, not essential to the "wait and see" tactic; and the observer soon learns to vary active stalking with passive waiting, stand-ing in shadows, sitting below foliage or next to a bush.

It is important to realize that unless you crash about like a buf-falo, even shy birds usually return quickly to the spot where you first saw them. So a quiet wait by a sunny, sheltered wood-edge or looking out onto a wide estuary will always be more productive than a trample through undergrowth or a wander along a skyline.

Do not forget your own comfort and ease of movement when approaching birds. To experience cramp, chattering teeth or a sweat drop in the eye just as an unusual bird finally comes out for inspection is no way to end a hunt. One useful tip is to have your pockets almost empty and keep notebooks, etc. in a zippered bag on your waist belt. I use an old skiing holdall and it is big enough to hold compass, paintbox, water bottle and all. Unlike the always tedious rucksack, I never feel it even at the end of a long day.

Learning how to stalk

Your first stalking ground should be a large garden or a public park. There your quarry will be used to human traffic and the errors in your stalking will be kept down to a toler-able level. Please don't start with a long chase after wild geese: save them for when you are really skilled.

First pick a target bird or flock, then work out the "most covered way" to it (by judging the presence and angles of trees, bushes, fences, etc.) and then work slowly along it (don't just walk, because you must constantly check that you are screened). Remember that effective cover need not hide you com-pletely; the trick is to mask your own tell-tale silhouette. Don't crouch or crawl from the word go; such post-ures can restrict your vision and should only be used when a really close approach is essential. Always keep your eye on your target and maintain a steady pace (never rush across gaps between cover). At all times, beware of scaring birds or mammals between you and the target. Their noisy alarm is likely to ruin your stalk. Guard particularly against the snapped branch or twig. Remember, too, to pick not just a

Keep the light behind you

④

Feeding thrushes and fieldfares

③

②

(1) When crossing an open space, walk slowly and avoid sudden movements, then (2) check the state of the birds from behind cover. (3) This is an excellent final watch point, close to the birds and with light behind you. (4) An impossible final watch point as crossing the gap from (3) will flush the birds.

①

target bird but also the best point for observing it, planning to have the light behind you whenever possible.

Once your skill begins to grow, try stalking in more and more open ground and learn to use every scrap of cover and fold in the land. The golden rule in wide, flat landscapes is to avoid the skyline at all costs, even if it means going the long way round. Use patience and cunning when you pit your wits against the greatest escapers of the animal kingdom.

How to wait and see

To appreciate fully the marvels that come from patient, still observation, you should pick a place well fre-

quented by birds, find a spot (on its edge) to spy on it, and then just wait – binoculars at the ready. It is always possible to do this on foot but standing can get tiring. So do not forget how useful a car can be as a mobile hide. I look out of my car window more and more; and in October 1980, I saw an American Wigeon – new in across the Atlantic – on a roadside pool near my home.

The sorts of habitat that reveal most birds to a patient observer are the "suntrap" sheltered edges of mixed woodland, willow- and sallow-lined pools in farmland, and reedy marshes near rivers and estuaries. Always keep an eye open for such likely spots.

73

Seeing birds

Most of us take our sight for granted, but once you start birdwatching you will soon realize that unaided it is not powerful enough to identify birds at a distance. A century ago the shotgun bridged this gap and most identified birds were dead ones. Nowadays the optical equipment market blooms with a huge choice of glass and camera.

Few people contribute more to this market than birdwatchers. So beware the specious offers ("Ex navy, × 32, lets you read a newspaper at 1000 yards") and make your purchases wisely. Your first will be of binoculars; never buy them in the street outside the shop, only after actually looking at birds in natural habitat. Check them for sharp focus, a bright and correctly coloured image, handiness, robustness and availability of service. It is well worth taking along an experienced binocular user with you; and be especially firm about that field trial. If a retailer is reluctant you may need to leave a deposit. Always point out that you are making an important purchase because binoculars are a working tool that you will be using for many years: they therefore need a fair field trial.

Assuming they are optically correct, the ideal binoculars for birdwatching should have four further characteristics: high magnification, good light gathering power, a wide field of view and a fast method of focussing. Magnifications of 9 or 10 are favoured by most birdwatchers, so look especially at glasses with 9 × 35 to 10 × 40 specifications.

Your second purchase will probably be a telescope. A few years ago they were long, unwieldly and heavy but now they are short, compact and handier. To use one efficiently, you really need a tripod, and altogether the full kit constitutes quite a load. So invest in a telescope only if you are going to watch birds over long distances or wish to check appearance and behaviour very closely. Remember that such an instrument is inevitably a "narrow tube" with a poor field of view. In your purchase, aim always for a sharp, bright image

▼ To check your colour perception note the colours of a bird then compare your notes against a field guide.

Male chaffinch

throughout the visual range of 20 to 60 magnifications. Once again, do not buy without a proper field test.

These days many birdwatchers clank about with binoculars, telescope *and* camera, but I do not advise a camera for beginners. A reflex camera body and at least two good lenses (up to 500mm focal length) are expensive – and there is no point in contributing to the film processing industry until you are certain that a photographic record will assist your special interests.

Sadly there is no handy kit for enhancing your hearing, a sense with even more vagaries than sight. It is important that you test it for defects and adapt your approach accordingly, taking particular care to adopt a standard form of noting bird sounds. If songs and calls become a special interest, you will probably eventually want to buy a tape recorder and a directional microphone.

Testing your eyes

As well as developing a consistent style for noting bird sounds, you will need to practise recording colours precisely. In avian plumage and bare parts (bill, legs and feet), colours vary both widely and subtly.

One difficulty here is that the same colour is often seen quite differently by two people. Try describing two or three of your local species and comparing your notes against the texts (not the illustrations) in a field guide or handbook. Look out for any colours that you don't see properly. If there are many (particularly in the red band), you should take a colour card test with your doctor and so know the extent of any deficiency.

Aim too to settle on standard colour terms. One day you might be asked, "Was it brownish-grey or greyish-brown?" Being sure which tone it was may make or break an identification claim.

However good your eyesight, your final perception of birds is frequently subject to illusions. Light and shade do play tricks with colours and patterns so always try to double check your initial impression.

Keeping notes

One of the best things about bird-watching is the memories that you will have. By leafing through old notebooks, logbooks and sketch-books you can always relive great days with birds and, of course, the not-so-great days – the ones when you got soaked through, saw nothing *and* missed the last bus.

To start with, try regularly keeping notes and making sketches. You will soon begin to build up a real bank of information. Most birdwatchers are quite good at jotting down field notes, but why not take things a step further and write a narrative log? Your logbook can be a diary account of the day's events, with comments sketches and analysis.

The tools of the trade

For use in the field, I suggest you take a pocket-sized, well-bound notebook and a hard-backed, loose leaf sketchbook (fairly fine cartridge paper).

▼ **Below are the author's field notes on an unusual warbler. On the opposite page are sketches made on the spot. The illustration in the author's log (opposite below) was drawn from the notes and sketches and clinched the identification.**

strange _Phylloscopus_   22-9.80

Seen in sycamore canopy of Old Fall Plantation, Flamborough Hd.

1st found at 1000 hrs. and watched at 50, later only 20 yards for c. 30 minutes, through 10 x 40

attention initially attracted by piercing Coal Tit-like note – written seweet or seeveet – but bird soon lost, – refound by calls which allow-ed "tracking", as it fed incessantly in upper foliage

clearly small for a _Phylloscopus_, recalling Goldcrest in shape – showed shorter tail and less bulk than nearby Chiffchaff – flight fast and light, allowing hover (when searching undersurface of leaves)

noticeably pale below, with whit-ish underbody constantly catch-ing eye before any other mark – upperparts hidden at first but long supercilium very obvious, contrasting with dark eyestripe

when bird descended to lower branches, greenish upperparts showed strong pattern – quite unlike Chiffchaff or Willow War-bler – with obvious double wing-bar, with cream tips to greater

Smaller than
chiffchaff

distinctly green
above

"covered in
stripes"

pale tips
to tertials

?two
wing-bars

prominent
supercilium

occasionally
hovered

white
below

crown
slightly
paler
in
centre

Shape rather
compact—
not unlike
Goldcrest

thin bill
with pale
base

Sides of breast
with faint lines
or clouding

details of
folded wing
(close view)
— cream tips
to both median
and ar- ater
. lattw
ing
k

ries,
ps
res
's

strange *Phylloscopus*
sycamore canopy,
Old Fall plantation
Flamborough Head
1000 – 1030, 29-0 -
in sunl...

Yellow-browed Warbler
Phylloscopus inornatus
Old Fall, Flamborough Head
29 September 1980
identified from field notes
and sketches; finished draw-
ing matched to Handbook
description and plate
confusion species – Pallas's
P. proregulus clearly ruled
out by lack of golden crown
stripe and rump patch

77

The ideal logbook (you will be writing this up at home) is a hard-sided, spine-lock file with loose leaf paper. A file like this will give you space for up to five years' diary accounts and field note analysis.

Make the logbook the bible of your own observations and you will have an exciting store of memories and information that you will enjoy re-reading.

You will probably also need some companion files for record summaries (to be sent to your local society recorder), difficult identifications, particular studies and the like.

The important rule in notekeeping is to preserve not only the bare facts of counts and events but also your impressions and thoughts about them. If you can do this, your records will become a rich source for both imaginative and scientific analysis over many years. Hard as it is to write full notes after a long field day, they are the very stuff of field ornithology.

▼ Below and on the opposite page are examples of the kind of records and comments that can go into a logbook.

SCHEDULE
April 1960
Night migrants in Regent's Park

Date	4	5	6	7	8	9	10	11	4-11
Species									
Redwing	4			2					6
Wheatear					1	1	2		4
Chiffchaff					2	1	1		3+
Willow Warbler					9	18	5	3	10	25+
Goldcrest							1		1
ALL above 4	0	12	23	8	3	10			39+

Wind direction SW SE S SW SW SW WSW
Overnight rain √ √ gale √

NB Willow Warbler fall on 8th biggest in study so far; Goldcrest on same day first in spring. Totals for warblers indicate minimum numbers passing through in five days.

NARRATIVE

12 April 1960

Most of the day was spent in the Brecks and I didn't get into Regent's Park. A chance, however, to reflect on the recent falls of night migrants which though small by coastal observatory standards have been pronounced. The first influx on the 7th was two days later than in 1959 but the willow warbler count on the 8th was a spring record. As usual in spring, the warblers were all in lakeside trees and not scattered round the count route. In spite of the overnight rain and wind, the birds showed no strain and most sang as they fed. The chorus of willow warblers on the 8th almost drowned the traffic roar for once. The last fall of willow warblers on the 11th was surprising; they must have a hard time flying through the tail of the gale - but such is the purposefulness of summer visitors eager to breed that

GETTING TO KNOW BIRDS
Learning key species

You will soon come across birds that you don't recognize. Knowing something about the relationship of bird species and families will help you to identify the unfamiliar ones. Perhaps the easiest way to look at the relationships is to see them as a tree, with the first families that evolved forming the lower branches, and the most recently evolved families the higher branches. At the end of the family branches are the twigs or individual species.

In some cases there is only one species in a family. In Europe, the wren is a prime example of a well known bird standing alone as both family and species. Small, russet, with tail cocked, voice noisy and behaviour irascible, it leaves few people confused about its identity.

In most families, however, there are several, even many species, and these may show overlaps in appearance, voice and behaviour at all times or in non-breeding plumage. These constitute the pitfalls in bird identification and you will have to watch your step among them. Undoubtedly the easiest way to separate similar species is to study the commonest one fully, so that you can spot the others "by exception" and lose no time in seeing the small but significant field characters that establish their identity beyond doubt.

Examples of common *key species* are the fulmar and Manx shearwater (in the petrel tribe), the mallard and teal (in surface-feeding ducks), the kestrel (in falcons), and the dunlin and ringed plover (in small waders). These are all non-passerine birds.

In passerines (see opposite*), first targets are the skylark, the meadow pipit, the spotted flycatcher, and (in the mob of little brown jobs that make up the warblers) the reed, garden and willow warblers and the whitethroat.

▼ Female ducks of these three species can be confusing. Note the subtle differences in the head shape and bill colour of the gadwall and in the speculum colour of the black duck.

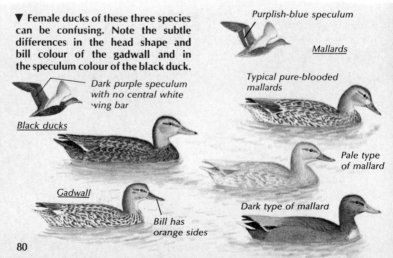

Purplish-blue speculum

Mallards

Dark purple speculum with no central white wing bar

Typical pure-blooded mallards

Black ducks

Pale type of mallard

Gadwall

Dark type of mallard

Bill has orange sides

Sorting out female ducks

Do not set yourself too severe a start in key species learning. I suggest that you begin with female ducks (see opposite) in a local waterfowl collection or on a gravel pit. Happily they are quite large birds and you can usually get good views of them.

The very common female mallard makes an excellent first subject. Not only is it similar to the female gadwall but it also sports unusual individuals which resemble various domestic strains and the rare black duck from America. Even experts are confused by funny-looking mallards, so get to know them as well as you can. Once you have done this, you can move confidently onto the stiffer puzzles of distinguishing female teal from garganey and the rarer vagrant teals. It took me 30 years to sort these out!

Separating small finches

Once you have cracked the problems of separating some groups of large birds, you can face the even tougher puzzles posed by small passerines.

One common and crucial key species is the linnet, an open country finch only too often confused – in female and immature plumages – with its upland cousin the twite and its woodland relative the redpoll. Take care: their appearances (see below) and some of their calls overlap dangerously. A mixed migrant flock of all three species, as I have seen on Fair Isle, can be the devil to sort out. Meet their challenge and your identification skills will be well established.

▼ Females of these three finches are very similar. To distinguish them, look closely at head and wing patterns.

Red forehead

Clear white wing bars

Whitish wing patch

Redpolls

Black chin

Faint white wing bars

Linnets

Twites

Pale straw bill

Reading habitat

The art of "reading" habitat is to look at a landscape and pick out the features that will attract particular birds. Generally birds frequent most those habitats which support them best in terms of cover (for shelter and safety) and food (for energy). Every bird species also selects the best possible site for nesting.

Competition between species has made some of these habitat preferences sharply defined. During the seasons of migration and in hard weather, the choices of habitat may be temporarily disrupted. Even then, however, birds search for and usually find the vegetation or piece of ground that yields the best immediate living.

Generally, the more diverse the habitat (and the plants and food sources within it), the more varied its bird life. Each type of habitat has its own typical species known as a "profile". A read of your field guide will arm you with profiles of species that can be expected in woods, on heaths, and so on. What the books often don't tell you, however, is how certain plants and certain habitat interfaces provide the best chances for a close study of birds. (Habitat interfaces are junctions where two or more habitats meet.)

Which plants are best for birds will depend on which species you are looking for. The always delightful warblers, for example, favour deciduous trees and their insect life; so if you are after warblers, take a good look at any group of willows, sallows or sycamores. Particularly in

Sparrowhawk

Mixed woods

Ash

Willow tit at stream edge

Willow warbler in sallow

Conifers

Sallows

Field edge

Stream

Linnet

Broken-down hawthorn

Weeds

Red-legged partridges

Field track

late autumn, these trees may sport not just the common chiffchaff but also the rare yellow-browed warbler, a vagrant from Siberia.

Habitat interfaces have a lot of birds because here species from different habitats meet. A slack backwater of a big river, for instance, bordered by rushes and sallows, will attract birds ranging from tits and warblers to rails, ducks and unusual waders. A careful stalk past such an area is always worthwhile and it will also be a good spot to wait-and-see.

Finding bird-rich habitats in farmland
Five thousand years ago the European countryside was largely broad-leaved, deciduous woodland, but farming has modified it. Today's

agricultural quilt is a patchwork, dominated by changing cropland. Scattered within this are barer high tops, woods and plantations, ancient heaths and (sadly) fewer and fewer wetlands.

Where these non-agricultural features do occur, there are miles and miles of habitat interfaces and strips along which at least two profiles of

▼ The habitat interface of harvest-time fields and woods in the author's study area. Forming an interface with the fields and woods is a stream, and inset are two species it attracts. In late summer, as the bird population reaches its peak, the open ground of the fields and the sunny shelter of the woods will support both resident and migrant species.

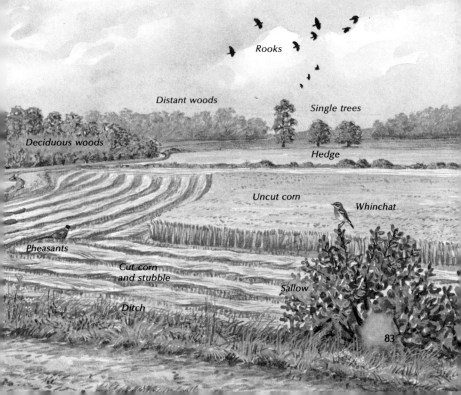

Rooks

Distant woods

Single trees

Deciduous woods

Hedge

Uncut corn

Whinchat

Pheasants

Cut corn and stubble

Sallow

Ditch

83

Distant woods

Woodpigeons

Open grass

Short-eared owl

Fence

Plough

Skylarks

Reed buntings

Yellowhammers

Redpolls

species abut and often intermingle. Birdwatching along such places is always more interesting than that allowed by plodding through uniform habitats.

The interfaces may be very obvious, as where a wood edge with a stream meets hedge-rimmed fields, or less obvious, as where a weedy (seed-bearing) boundary to a road offers relatively more shelter and food than tarmac and stubble.

Try to pick out bird productive areas, spotting them first from a meandering car and then checking them on foot. Having a short list of, say, five such places will speed any survey. The illustrations show one interface (pages 82–83) and one strip (above) that I regularly search in my own study area. Always be ready for the really unusual bird to pop up along such habitat edges. Even well inland, they can provide exciting encounters with migrants.

Trial and error will show you how

A frequent winter scene in farmland, near the author's home in North Humberside. A snowfall has disturbed the normal distribution of birds and they are intent on finding food from every source. Note how a weedy verge – a habitat strip – can be suddenly full of finches and buntings. Two birds of prey – short-eared owl and kestrel – are also looking for food.

Kestrel

Distant woods

Lapwings

Fence

Snow cover

Buntings

Weeds

Yellowhammer

Ditch

Weeds

Grass verge

Rooks

Chaffinch

to read a landscape ornithologically. A first scan over a new area should be a mouth-watering experience. Learn to think ahead and you won't be wasting time by blundering about. You'll see a lot more birds and have a good chance of finding an unusual species or two.

Studying birds in towns

If you live in a town or large city, bird habitats (and yours) will be few and much less natural. You will see fewer species but it will be fascinating to discover how far they have penetrated into the urban habitat. Magpies, for instance, have recently moved into central London (jays got there before them), herons are now breeding in Regent's Park and a pair of rooks nests within five miles of St. Paul's Cathedral. On and off I lived in inner London for 14 years and looking back, I found birdwatching there no less fulfilling than rarity-hunting in Scilly or on Fair Isle.

85

Exploring bird communities

Once you have worked up a know-ledge of key species and habitat pre-ferences, you will be well equipped to explore a bird community. The annual cycle of birds is dominated by the activities of summer repro-duction and winter survival. The full story of these will start to emerge if you watch a diverse population through the course of a year.

Finding a bird community
Every piece of habitat attracts its own birds; so it will be best if you can find an area with a variety of cover and cultivation. This "study area" should be fairly small (200 to 300 acres) with clear boundaries so that you can view it as self-contained. It could be a city park, two or three suburban streets, the parkland centre of an estate or the surround of a lake or reservoir. If you can see the whole area from some point it will help but it isn't essential.

To start with, pick an area close to your home so that you can get to it easily. Try to visit it at least once a month through the year, or more often if you can.

Getting to know your birds
Observing a bird community will give you the chance to use all your skills of identification, stalking,
note-keeping and reading habitat.

One of the most interesting things you will discover is how birds use the habitat available to them (often man-made habitats that they share with us). Which areas do they choose for feeding, drinking, preen-ing, displaying, nesting and roost-ing? Why do they choose these areas rather than others? What do these areas offer them – is it food, shelter, safety, or perhaps something else?

You will see all kinds of fascinating behaviour. How, for instance, does a lapwing preen the back of its head? Well, it stands on one leg, raises the opposite wing to the horizontal and brings its free leg over the top of this wing, at the same time inclining its head backwards. Then it has a good scratch – lovely to see, hard to sketch, and it raises all sorts of ques-tions. Does it always use its right foot? Do other waders preen in the same way?

As you wander through your study area, take time to stop and stare. Make notes whenever you can and jot down your comments, questions, and impressions.

▼ To explore your local bird commun-ity stroll along a regular route through different habitats. Illustrated here and opposite are scenes you might find.

Skylarks and linnets concentrated on the less grassy patches of a foot-ball pitch. Why? Because the studs of football boots have broken up the turf and exposed an easy har-vest of seeds.

Mallards feeding along the edge of a lake, with tufted ducks in the open water. Why? Because mallards are mainly surface feeders and tufted ducks are under-water feeders. Both can therefore co-exist and breed on the same water.

Gulls roosting on an inland reservoir. Why not on fields? Because gulls are still essentially seabirds, wary of resting at night on land. By living in flocks they benefit from shared success in food searches.

A sparrowhawk pouncing on finches feeding near roost bushes. Why didn't it hover like a kestrel? Because round-winged hawks have developed a "close-quarter" hunting strategy designed for bird prey, not small mammals.

IDEAS FOR FIELDWORK

Studying a roost

The word "murmuration" means "a flock of starlings" and it really does sum up the busy hum of starlings as they fly in to roost.

The huge murmuration that nightly descends into Trafalgar Square, London is perhaps the best known gathering of birds in Britain. These starlings come in to roost from the whole circumference of the city and alternate sleep and chatter all night long. Generally speaking, however, our knowledge of roosting behaviour is thin and bitty. You could change this situation. So why not choose to study one of your local bird roosts?

Assessing the roost

The first step is to spy out the most likely sites, by finding and mapping the safe and sheltered coverts. Evergreens, hawthorns and rhododendrons are usually favoured, but don't ignore reed-beds and any other dense cover. The second step is to watch the sites during at least the last hour of daylight and discover which attracts birds. The third is to stand quietly by the roosts and identify and count the incoming species (see the logbook record on page 90). You will need to heighten your perception of bird calls to do this fully, since at dusk all roost arrivals tend to look like showers of black blobs. The fourth task is to stand back from the roost and try to trace the source of the incoming birds. This is not easy but it is worth a special effort,

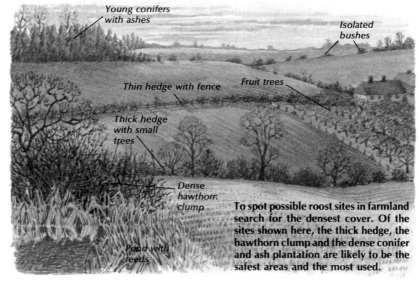

Young conifers with ashes

Isolated bushes

Thin hedge with fence

Fruit trees

Thick hedge with small trees

Dense hawthorn clump

Pond with reeds

To spot possible roost sites in farmland search for the densest cover. Of the sites shown here, the thick hedge, the hawthorn clump and the dense conifer and ash plantation are likely to be the safest areas and the most used.

since it will immediately link one piece of behaviour to another. It may even tempt you up before dawn to watch the roost break up and the birds commute back in the direction from which they came.

If you can watch the roost on a regular basis you will see interesting changes in numbers and possibly in the species using it.

Surprises

As always, be ready for the occasional excitement such as a tawny owl trying for an easy meal or, as I once saw, a great grey shrike looking menacingly down at some dozy redpolls. And don't forget to send in notes on your roost watches to the local society. Few current birdwatchers bother; so your local recorder should be delighted by your special interest.

Next incoming group

Skeletal trees

Incoming greenfinches

Quiet observer

Dense hawthorn

Greenfinches

Thick brambles

Counting the incoming birds at a roost. Some roost sites hold only one species, others attract several species. Note the type of roost cover each species favours. Numbers may vary from day to day and there will certainly be seasonal changes.

▼ A logbook record of incoming birds at a communal roost. Weather conditions and light affect roosting time. Notes on the type of cover each species uses will help you locate other roosts. The nearby rook and jackdaw roost would be worth studying. Are there other flight lines to it?

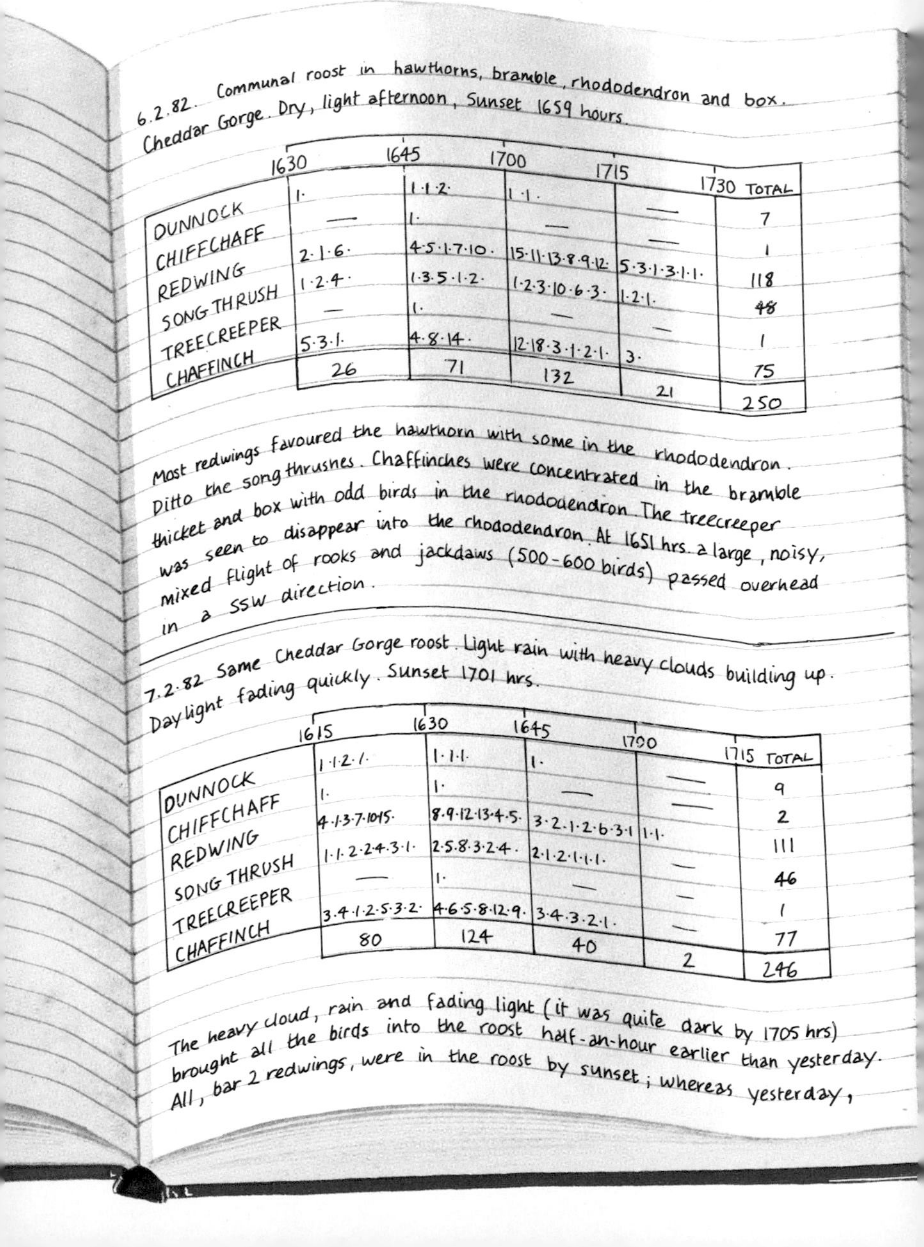

6.2.82. Communal roost in hawthorns, bramble, rhododendron and box. Cheddar Gorge. Dry, light afternoon, Sunset 1659 hours.

	1630	1645	1700	1715	1730	TOTAL
DUNNOCK	1·	1·1·2·	1·1·	—	—	7
CHIFFCHAFF		1·				1
REDWING	2·1·6·	4·5·1·7·10·	15·11·13·8·9·12·	5·3·1·3·1·1·		118
SONG THRUSH	1·2·4·	1·3·5·1·2·	1·2·3·10·6·3·	1·2·1·		48
TREECREEPER	—	1·				1
CHAFFINCH	5·3·1·	4·8·14·	12·18·3·1·2·1·	3·		75
	26	71	132	21		250

Most redwings favoured the hawthorn with some in the rhododendron. Ditto the song thrushes. Chaffinches were concentrated in the bramble thicket and box with odd birds in the rhododendron. The treecreeper was seen to disappear into the rhododendron. At 1651 hrs a large, noisy, mixed flight of rooks and jackdaws (500-600 birds) passed overhead in a SSW direction.

7.2.82 Same Cheddar Gorge roost. Light rain with heavy clouds building up. Daylight fading quickly. Sunset 1701 hrs.

	1615	1630	1645	1700	1715	TOTAL
DUNNOCK	1·1·2·1·	1·1·1·	1·	—	—	9
CHIFFCHAFF	1·	1·	—			2
REDWING	4·1·3·7·1015·	8·9·12·13·4·5·	3·2·1·2·6·3·1·	1·1·		111
SONG THRUSH	1·1·2·2·4·3·1·	2·5·8·3·2·4·	2·1·2·1·1·1·	—		46
TREECREEPER		1·				1
CHAFFINCH	3·4·1·2·5·3·2·	4·6·5·8·12·9·	3·4·3·2·1·	—		77
	80	124	40	2		246

The heavy cloud, rain and fading light (it was quite dark by 1705 hrs) brought all the birds into the roost half-an-hour earlier than yesterday. All, bar 2 redwings, were in the roost by sunset; whereas yesterday,

Mapping starling flight lines

The bird roost champion of Europe is probably the starling. It forms enormous assemblies at dusk and these swarms – sometimes numbered in millions – spend the night in sheltered places. In open country, starlings mostly choose dense plantations or reedbeds to roost in but in this century, their suburban and urban cousins have clearly worked out that the centres of cities offer both warmth and safety.

The large starling roost on buildings and trees in and around Trafalgar Square, London was the subject of a major piece of research 30 years ago. The map below shows how the amateur observers of the London Natural History Society defined the length and direction of the flight lines of incoming starlings over the entire London area. You could do similar research in your home area and hunt out your local starling roost and the flight lines to it.

Plotting flight lines

When you see small flocks of starlings in the evening, plot a line on the map showing their direction of flight. By moving to different places on other evenings you can begin to plot several flight lines. The roost should be located where these lines meet. It will take some time and effort to define all the flight lines and how far they extend and this is probably best done with a team of people. It would be interesting, though – with the help of a car or bike – to follow one flight line yourself, to see just how far the birds fly to the roost.

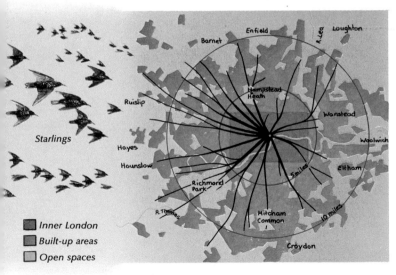

▲ The 1952 map showing starling flight lines (in black) to the central roosts in and near Trafalgar Square, London. Some birds flew 14 miles to roost.

Looking at tits feeding

Tits have long been the favourites of behavioural scientists, with the birds' seemingly clever and certainly acrobatic antics and relative tameness. But there is always something new to be learnt about these colourful birds. For example, how do the six common species (blue, great, coal, marsh, willow and long-tailed tit) coexist in your local woods? One way to answer this question would be to observe closely their food searches to see which trees and plants they feed on and at what heights they are feeding.

During my winter exploration of Epping Forest in 1971/72, I noticed that the blue tit was present everywhere and was (presumably) the commonest tit. It clearly found some food in most vegetation and all the way up from the forest floor to the topmost twigs of beeches. How about finding out if it feeds in this way in your area?

How to survey
The first step is to find a typical piece of mature mixed woodland (including both deciduous and coniferous

▼ Watching a tit flock. Identify the different species and count them. Then note the span of height used by each species and the type of vegetation they are feeding in. Plot this information onto a map or record sheet.

Coal tit

Blue tit

Long-tailed tit

trees) that harbours tits. The second is to explore it fully and track the normal rounds of tits within it. The third is to construct a precise form for your observations. Divide the wood into areas of different vegetation, depending on the plant species, their densities and their heights. The illustration below shows a simple diagrammatic way of doing this. The fourth task is to choose several regular paths through the wood and count and map (by site and height) all the tits that you encounter along them.

Keep separate records of each species to see how they differ.

Working at, say, fortnightly intervals, your data will soon build up and your perception will grow too. The fifth and most mentally stimulating step is to analyse your records month by month to see how the changing vegetation affects where the tits feed. It could be that even the experts will learn from you. Incidentally you will never be bored in a wood, for even if the tits are absent, it will be the turn of a nuthatch or woodpecker to delight you.

▼ Final analysis of blue and great tit feeding heights in Black Plantation, from January to March 1982.

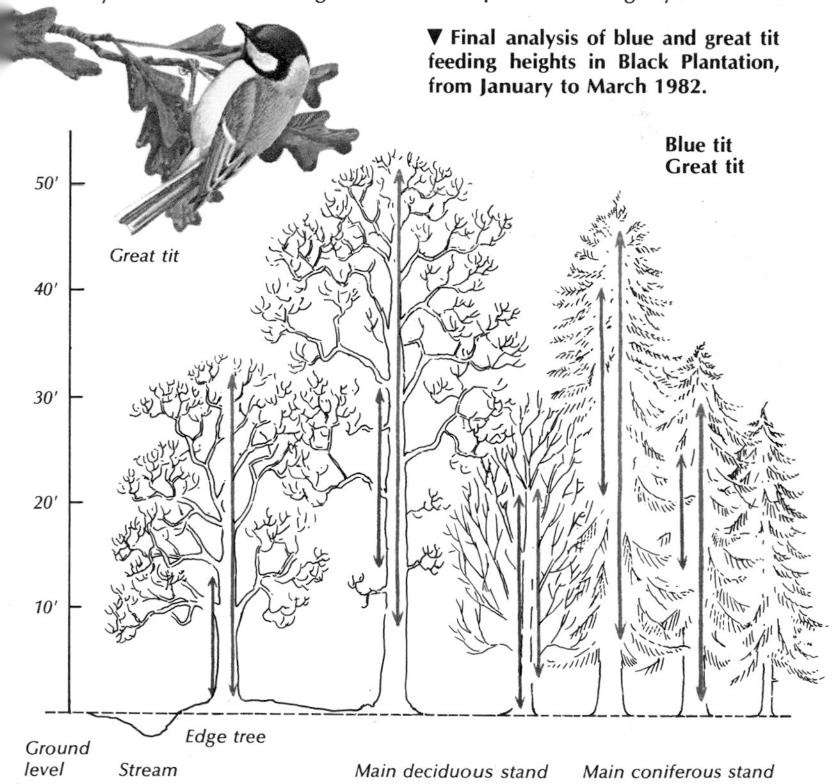

Blue tit
Great tit

Great tit

50'
40'
30'
20'
10'

Ground level
Stream
Edge tree
Main deciduous stand
Main coniferous stand

How does wind affect birds?

So envious are we of the flight of birds, we tend to believe that they have total mastery of airspace. This is not true, however, and strong, particularly blustery wind clearly inhibits wing action and aerial behaviour.

Surprisingly, I can think of no sustained study on the effect of strong wind on birds. I have tried to assess it when watching the coastal passage of seabirds and it seemed that given a wind force (on the Beaufort Scale) of 8 or above, even totally pelagic (ocean-living) species begin to have problems in maintaining station and direction.

Indeed, to watch such majestic birds as gannets turn and run before the wind is an awesome spectacle, worth seeing for the sight alone. Of course, birds surrounded by land can avoid wind stress simply by land-

Gannets turning to fly with the wind

Wind direction
→

Watching seabirds in a gale. At what wind speed do birds turn and fly with the wind rather than continue battling into it? Does poor visibility or rain make them turn at lower wind speeds?

ing and clinging onto something, but how strong does the wind have to be to stop them flying? And if it is raining, as well, do they stop flying sooner?

Working out the effect of wind stress
You could test these questions on two common summer visitors, the swallow and the house martin. Both of these birds feed on insects caught in flight, so they are ideal for this study.

Here are a few clues on how to start. First, get hold of a copy of the Beaufort Scale which will show you how to judge wind speed. Second, tune into the shipping forecast (on BBC Radio 4 at 0625, 1350 and 1750 hours) to find out when gales are forecast. You should be able to judge from the nearest sea area if gales are going to hit your part of the country. Third, go to a habitat where swallows or house martins feed (ponds, cricket pitches and farmyards are often good spots). Fourth, watch the birds tussle with the rising wind and note down what you see.

Check the wind speed regularly and see how this affects the birds' feeding activity. Are they feeding in an open area or using the shelter of trees and buildings? Are the birds flying low? Do they perch now and again or fly all the time? Watching their behaviour closely you will probably come up with all sorts of other questions. Are there, in fact, any insects on the wing in a Force 7 wind?

Do some background reading on bird behaviour if you can, as you'll find that knowing some of the answers will lead you to ask the right questions.

Windy weather

Barn lee

Swallows feeding in the lee of a barn where they get some shelter from the wind. How strong does the wind have to be to stop them flying?

Observing migration

Bird migration is the only mass animal movement that we regularly see, now that Europe has lost its droves of wild mammals. It is a phenomenon that is both quite astonishing and easily understood.

Bird migration is astonishing because we have to accept that birds as small as goldcrests (weighing just a few grams and with a pea-sized brain) can successfully fly over both cold mountains and stormy seas. We also have to accept that they – and all their migrant companions, from the closely related firecrests to wild swans – have inherited navigation systems which enable them to find and refind both their summer and winter homes. (Thus my own pair of swallows fly unerringly between my stable and a South African reedbed.) All these unlikely propositions have now been confirmed by extensive research, but after 40 years' experience of bird migration, I still find it totally enthralling.

Bird migration is, however, fully understandable, since it is a reflection of the seasonal ebb and flow in the food supply. As long as this food source fluctuates, then birds will react to its changes and pounce on every opportunity offered to them, whether for summer reproduction or winter survival.

The basic rhythm and some of the dimensions of bird migration were first spotted 5000 years ago but it is only in the last 30 years that ornithologists have fully demonstrated just how far birds can travel. Given their powers of flight, energy conservation and navigation, birds can shift almost from pole to pole and (in temperate latitudes) across a third of the world's circumference!

Types of migration

With such a complex phenomenon, it is not sensible to generalize too much but in most of Europe, various types of bird migration are broadly separable and can be studied by a selection of techniques and tactics.

The most obvious migratory movements are the arrival and departure of locally breeding summer visitors, the passage (generally north in spring and south in autumn) of high latitude summer visitors, the arrival and departure of winter visitors (escaping from the extremer continental climate to the east), occasional irruptions (of species suddenly become numerous or

▲ Many birds migrate unseen at night.

faced with a food shortage), the overshooting of low latitude summer visitors, and the vagrancy of Asian and American birds.

On the western seaboard of Europe – and nowhere more so than in Britain – all these movements can become suddenly visible. Bird-watchers have learnt to look out particularly for weather conditions that produce migrants. These can be anticyclones and easterly winds that allow birds to drift west across northern Europe; warm, wet southerlies that push others north from the Mediterranean; and howling westerlies (born of Caribbean hurricanes) that blow yet others across the Atlantic.

Redstarts

Study techniques

The study of bird migration was most popular in the 1950s and 1960s and its study methods were most refined then. Essentially they combine two disciplines, a daily estimate of birds both grounded in or moving over a clearly delimited recording area and a related sample of birds trapped in the same area or in other areas where summer visitors are concentrated. The captured birds are measured and weighed, examined for moult and other physiological conditions and then ringed in the hope that they will be recovered at another point along their route or retrapped later at the same site.

Trapping, examination in the hand and ringing require lengthy training and you must have a permit (from a national authority such as the British Trust for Ornithology). It is illegal to "have a go"; so please do not. (See pages 110–112 for places to observe trapping and ringing.) In your first years, you should concentrate on the counting discipline and experiment with it in various habitats.

Bird migration is most clearly seen along hillsides, across water and on coastlines. It is most dramatic on promontories and offshore or oceanic islands but in the following pages I deal mainly with inland observation techniques.

This map shows some of the movements of birds over Europe.

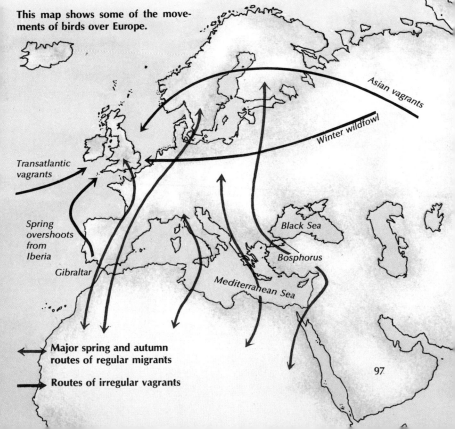

Transatlantic vagrants

Spring overshoots from Iberia

Gibraltar

Asian vagrants

Winter wildfowl

Black Sea

Bosphorus

Mediterranean Sea

→ **Major spring and autumn routes of regular migrants**

→ **Routes of irregular vagrants**

97

Counting migrants on the ground
During your first exploration of a bird community, you are likely to experience at least one marked arrival of migrants. Suddenly among your resident species, there will be a flush of warblers, a swirl of finches or thrushes, or, to mention a scarcer bird, a green sandpiper exploding out of a ditch.

To assess such arrivals and the subsequent departures as precisely as possible, you must first pick a sampling area or map out a counting route. Then walk through this area or along the route as often as possible – daily just after dawn is favourite – and count every bird present. Take care too to note the weather and any other associated event. By transposing your counts and notes to a daily register, you will soon develop a measure of the bird migration in your area. Examples of a logbook record of grounded migrants appear on pages 78–79.

I shall be surprised if you do not succumb to the pleasant fever of migration study within a week of starting your daily search.

▼ **Migrants fly lower and are most visible when flying into or across a headwind. Here the majority of birds (97%) were flying W to NW into NW and N winds. Peak numbers occurred shortly after sunrise, tailing off as the sky clouded over.**

6 November 1960 Primrose Hill, London.

Wind NW, then N, force 2-3; sky clear at dawn but clouding over, 8/8 cloud by 1000.

Sunrise 0735. Usual mile front as count base.

Not cold.   h = heard not seen.

¼ hour counts starting at	0715	0730	0745	0800	0815	species total
WOODPIGEON	30 W 20 W	20 WNW 75 W 80 W	275 W 175 NW 16 W	42 w	6 W	739
SKYLARK			1 W	h 2 W 1 W 1w h	h	8+
FIELDFARE	12 NW 2 W	25 WNW 5 NW	3 W			47
SONG THRUSH	5 WNW				1 W	6
CHAFFINCH	7 W h	2 NWh 4 NW 2 N Wh	4 NW 1 NW h	h 5NW h 5 W h	h 1 W 3. WNW 1N 2 NW	45+
GREENFINCH		1 NW 2 NW 3 WNW	h 1 N		3 NWh 2 NW 3 W	17+
GOLDFINCH	1 W		2 WNW	1 W		4
HOUSE SPARROW	2W	6 W	4w	4 SW		16
TREE SPARROW	5 W	1 w	2 W			8
STARLING	120 WNW 18 NW 21 SW	20 NW 15 NW	1 NW 30 NW 27 NW	12 WNW 150 NW 4 NW	5W	423
Grand totals	244	263+	544+	232+	30+	1,313+

definitely on the move!

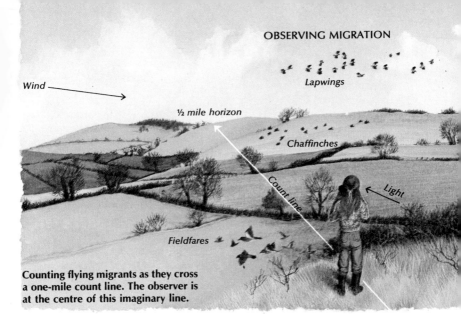

Wind

Lapwings

½ mile horizon

Chaffinches

Count line

Light

Fieldfares

Counting flying migrants as they cross a one-mile count line. The observer is at the centre of this imaginary line.

Counting migrants in the sky

Again, during your early fieldwork there will probably be an autumn day when the sky is unusually full of birds, perhaps lapwings in twinkling flocks or fieldfares in harshly chuckling parties. The day may also be one of low cloud and northwesterly wind, the last forcing the birds to fly into it and "keep their heads down".

Getting a full quantitative measure of such movements is impracticable but obtaining a qualitative sample is well worthwhile. Your first task is to find an uncluttered viewpoint, such as an isolated hill, a valley shoulder or an open horizon.

Your second task is to establish a fixed count line (see the illustration above). Ideally this line should be a mile long (half a mile in front of you and half a mile behind you) but its length will actually be determined by the limits of your flight identification expertise. (You will need to work hard on basic plumage

patterns, flight actions and calls.)

The third job is to count all the birds passing over the count line, noting the flight direction of each flock, as in the table on the left. If you count "all" the birds passing over a mile front for one hour, you will get a total of "birds per mile per hour". You can work out passage rates for individual species on the same basis. These standard measurements make it easy to compare counts from different days.

You can also assess the directions of passage of different species over your count line. Never pretend to see all the birds in the sky; concentrate most on a qualitative sample and you will soon learn what birds are flying over your area. Believe me, it is great fun. Dawn watches from Primrose Hill in London in the 1960s brought me staggering flights of thousands of woodpigeons and wonderful single birds like a lost Bewick's swan and an osprey!

99

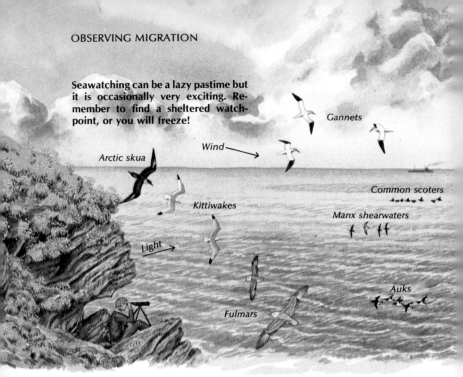

Seawatching can be a lazy pastime but it is occasionally very exciting. Remember to find a sheltered watchpoint, or you will freeze!

Gannets

Arctic skua

Wind

Common scoters

Kittiwakes

Manx shearwaters

Light

Auks

Fulmars

Watching seabird passage

As a change from the routine of inland observations, there is nothing more refreshing than a long watch over a stream of seabirds. Seawatching, as the technique is called, is a recent invention and was first developed at the most famous of Irish bird observatories, Cape Clear Island in County Cork.

What you can see on a seawatch will depend on the weather, the angle of the light (it needs to be behind you) and your height above the sea (if you are too close to sea level you will miss birds further out).

When you first start you will need some guidance from experienced seawatchers. They will be able to give you a lot of tips, particularly on identification and how to locate birds at sea. Seawatching is an art

and it will take time to pick it up. The excitements can be huge but the risks of mistaken identifications are enormous.

Seabirds are made most visible during onshore gales and tend to be concentrated in passage streams where a headland or coastline angle interrupts the normally broad front dispersal of birds offshore.

So before any first attempt, you should study a map of your nearest coast and pick your watchpoint to allow a maximum of back light and your greatest extension into the water mass. Then wait for when the wind blows onshore – for example, NW to SW on west-facing coasts, NW to E on east-facing headlands or shorelines – and off you go, remembering that a dawn start is the only way not to miss something good.

25 September 1976
Flamborough Head and Bridlington Bay

ENE/ESE 6-8
Rain to 1245

I went straight to the head but apart from large rain, I could see nothing moving at sea and only the odd chat round the carpark. So I wandered off in the car to check a few hedge lees, finding Redstarts, Wheatears and, surprisingly, many Reed Buntings. A Ruff stumbled through the deluge which was so constant that I almost gave up and went home. A lucky stop at North Bay at 0950 soon convinced me that I should stay, for suddenly seabirds were pouring past just offshore. Clearly the near gale and poor visibility was "trapping" them against the coast and forcing them to turn back east under the southern cliffs. I watched from the shelter of the car for three hours with absolutely splendid results and adrenalin surge after adrenalin surge. It wa... ...lin surge ...do with the weather: low squall... ...ight, and the birds coming N, ...out to E. At 1245 the weath... ...hurried back to the he... ...e was still obvious. A... ...t the "sea bird eva... ...t back ...s... ...inutes ...was ...a ...g

25 September 1976 Flamborough Head and Bridlington Bay

	North Bay 0950-1245	Head 1300-1450	North Bay 1515-1545	All birds moving into NE/E gale, unless as stated
Red-throated Diver	2			
Fulmar	1 +?1	1	5	
Cory's Shearwater	2		3	
large Shearwater	6	30		
Sooty Shearwater	1	35		
Balearic Shearwater		1		
Leach's Petrel	36	10		
Gannet	5	1		
Wigeon	53			included incredible flock of 50! with Grey Plover flock
Scoter	15			
Goosander	12	2	1	
Grey Plover	3	13		2 with Grey Plover flock
Knot	3	7		
Ruff		36		
Redshank		1		
Bar-tailed Godwit	4 +?1	7	40	7 immatures
Great Skua	68	26	3	at least 6 immatures up to 23 on sea
Pomarine Skua	6 +?2	150		
Arctic Skua	49	1		
Skua	390	2	5	
Long-tailed Skua		1		
Little Gull	8			
Kittiwake	75			P.S. White-winged Black Tern seen at head following my departure!
Sabine's Gull	11			
Black Tern	12			
Gull-billed Tern	21			
Sandwich Tern				
Common Tern				
Arctic Tern				

no sign of a Manx!

...pression of surges in passage at 1015-1023, 1115-1120, 1300-1320, 1400, 1500-1510 associated with brightest "light-break" and this "exposed" tubenoses behind those in, identifi... ...o knows what was miss...

25 September 1976 and Bridlington Bay Flamborough Head

▲ An account of a great seawatch, from the author's log.

Studying bird populations

▲ A male reed bunting singing to proclaim his territory.

Only 20 years ago few but professional ornithologists even attempted population studies – the foundations of bird conservation – but today tens of thousands of ordinary birdwatchers confidently contribute to them.

If you have already studied bird communities and migration (see pages 86–87 and 96–101) you will be well prepared for measuring bird populations. In most European countries, ornithologists and birdwatchers have already combined efforts to map the distribution of breeding birds, to sample their numbers, to assess the mass of vulnerable groups like seabirds, geese and waders, and (from 1981) to survey the distribution of wintering birds. In addition, there are current regional surveys of the birds of scarce habitats and a host of local studies. So the choice is wide and, in most cases, full instructions exist.

You must decide what kind of population study will interest you most, then set yourself clear objectives, choose a study area and relevant study methods, and finally make a long-term commitment to the most involving kind of birdwatching that there is.

Knowing how badly conservationists need more information on the fortunes of ordinary birds, I suggest that you attempt a population study close to your home and in three parts. Aim (1) to make a census of breeding birds, (2) to sample the arrival, passage and departure of migrants, and (3) to index the numbers of wintering birds. In this way, you will be able to see how birds ebb and flow through even a small piece of ground. The rest of this section explains how to do this.

Choosing a study area

If you have let this book guide you step by step, you should already have your eye on a likely study area. If you have not, look back at page 86 and note the way of spotting one. This time round, take into account the general approach summarized above and try to select an area (and its habitat balance) that are typical of the landscape in which you live. Your study results will then be broadly relevant to the wider ornithology of your region.

Mapping a study area

You will need to use large scale maps so that you can define the boundaries of your study area and see what different habitats it has. In Britain, for example, there is a 6":1 mile (1:10,560) series of amazing detail. This is the ideal size to use when selecting an area for study, as boundaries, buildings etc., can be clearly seen. For actually plotting the positions of birds you will normally need a larger scale Ordnance Survey map of 25":1 mile (1:2534).

Provided you update it with any major changes to buildings, hedges and woodlands, your local 25" sheet

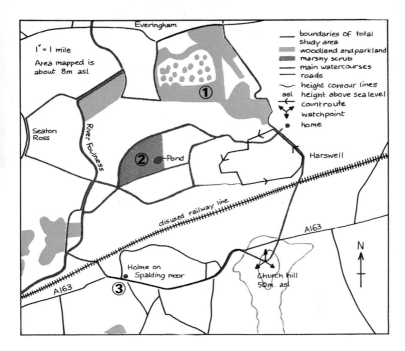

Everingham

1" = 1 mile
Area mapped is
about 8m asl

Seaton
Ross

River Foulness

①

② ● Pond

Harswell

disused railway line

A163

Holme on
Spalding moor ●

A163 ③

Church hill
50m. asl

N ↑

_____ boundaries of total
study area
▨▨▨ woodland and parkland
▓▓▓ marshy scrub
──── main watercourses
──── roads
⌒ height contour lines
asl height above sea level
↓ count route
↓ watchpoint
● home

▲ Try to choose a study area close to home. This map, of standard Ordnance Survey 1" scale, shows the author's study area 19 miles SE of York. Note (1) a large woodland area, (2) a last patch of wilderness and (3) the main village. All will support bird communities which are different from those in the surrounding farmland. CBC plots can be chosen in (1) and anywhere in the farmland.

will form an excellent plan for your study. You will need to keep a master copy – to record the habitat changes and uses – and at least 20 other copies on which to record bird positions and numbers. If you use coloured pens and symbols, do not forget to key them.

Taking a census of breeding birds
Various methods exist to establish the density of breeding birds but in order to make your results compatible with those of other birdwatchers, it is sensible to use that adopted by your national conservation body. In Britain, for example, it

is the Common Bird Census (CBC) which is administered by the British Trust for Ornithology (BTO).

Essentially the survey requires you to plot the precise positions of all singing, territorial male birds noted during spring and early summer in your study area. You may choose a farmland study area, for which at least 10 visits and an acreage of 200 (80 hectares) is the standard model, or a woodland one, for which 15 visits and 50 acres (20 hectares) is the usual requirement. To be of value to the BTO the survey should be carried out over a period of several years so that annual changes in

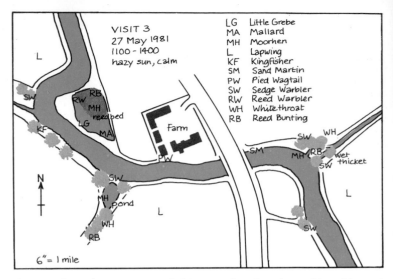

VISIT 3
27 May 1981
1100 - 1400
hazy sun, calm

LG	Little Grebe
MA	Mallard
MH	Moorhen
L	Lapwing
KF	Kingfisher
SM	Sand Martin
PW	Pied Wagtail
SW	Sedge Warbler
RW	Reed Warbler
WH	Whitethroat
RB	Reed Bunting

Farm

reedbed

wet thicket

pond

N

6" = 1 mile

▲ A map from the Waterways Bird Survey. Plotted on it are the positions of singing, territorial male birds, recorded on one visit.

breeding numbers can be compared.

The CBC is never complete – for a start, some birds are more easily missed than others – but it has been well tested since its inception in 1961 and is, therefore, widely quoted by conservation bodies. It is a survey well worth doing *providing* you have the time available.

If you have a particular interest in the birds of waterways, there is an alternative breeding birds census right up your street. It is the Waterways Bird Survey (see the map above) which, like the CBC, is organized by the BTO. This survey asks you to plot the whereabouts of over 50 species dependent on waterside habitats. The model performance is at least 9 searches of a 3-mile (5-kilometre) length. Full instructions on both surveys are available from the BTO (address on page 126).

Of course, you do not have to adopt the BTO methods. You may like to start with a simpler and quicker "straight line transect count". For this, plot a line across your study area and survey along it. This will provide a sample of the breeding birds in your study area, rather than a complete census.

Counting migrant birds

The various ways of counting migrant birds were discussed earlier, on pages 96–101. This time around, you have the chance to correlate your migrant counts made along a set route or through a selection of habitats with those made of breeding or wintering birds. Birds do not move only in spring and autumn. At least some do so on every day of the year. So there is always the chance of a surprise.

It makes sense to include your migrant count route with your CBC area but if there are other bird-rich habitats nearby, say a lake, a sewage farm (always good for birds) or an area of seasonal floods, frequent inspection of these will allow you to monitor a greater variety of species. Examples of the records that can be kept of migrant birds are shown on pages 78–79 and pages 98 and 101.

▲ Redwings are winter visitors whose numbers are affected by the weather.

Counting wintering birds

A standard method for assessing winter bird populations has not yet been set, though that chosen for survey work to produce a winter atlas (started in 1981 and organized by the BTO and Irish Wildbird Conservancy) may become the norm. So you are free to experiment with a method. I use a "broad transect count", not along a straight line but along a route that dissects or abuts all the main habitats in my study area. Inevitably the counts are incomplete but they do allow direct comparison, the crux of year-on-year methods.

Assessing the accuracy of your counts

The ability of birds to hide is remarkable, but they will often stay in food-bearing habitat for quite some time. As you count them, you must resist the temptation to forsake your standard route or search area in order to obtain a full list on every visit. Remember that you are building up long-term data. For all the methods noted above, the best checks are provided by an expert companion who has experience of the CBC and like surveys.

In my opinion, it takes about three years to understand how birds exploit a piece of mixed habitat and about seven to observe all the regular fluctuations in a bird community caused by short term climate changes, general population trends and other external factors.

Sending in your results

Most ornithological reporting is done on an annual cycle. In Britain, for example, the BTO will want your CBC report at the end of the summer. It will be analysed by computer and become part of the national index of 59 species. Given its recent commitment to a winter atlas, the BTO will also be interested in your winter survey.

All your results should be summarised and sent to your local bird recorder or the regional organiser of national surveys. A task for the long nights of January! No need to faint at the prospect, however, as both the people just mentioned will give you plenty of advice on format and content. You must observe one golden rule – always list your notes on species in systematic order – and if you want to demonstrate particular events, send copies of your notes or counts as well. In this way, the various editors using your data will not miss the significant additions to knowledge that you have made.

Learning from bird books

Today there are thousands more active birdwatchers than there were 30 years ago. This increase in field activity has greatly increased our knowledge of birds. If you want to keep in touch and have a good background knowledge you will need to read widely. So here is a guide to the types of book and journal available (more details on pages 126–127).

Stonechat

▲ Typical field guide illustrations.

Field guides

By now you will probably have bought a good "field guide". Field guides deal with identification. They contain illustrations of perched and flying birds and show various plumages of each species. The short text concentrates on information that will help identify the bird, giving details of size, plumage, calls, habitat and distribution. Some field guides cover all the birds of Europe, while others concentrate on British birds or a selection of the commonest species.

A field guide is one book that you must own, because without it you will find your way to the naming of families and species long and tortuous. Amongst the comprehensive Europe-wide guides, I suggest that you choose between "Peterson" and "Fitter" (to use their well-

known nicknames). A useful guide to the commoner British species is Rob Hume's *Usborne Guide to Birds*, which is well illustrated with good pointers on identification.

Local bird reports

Detailed information on local birds will appear in the annual report published by the ornithological society or naturalists' trust of your county or province. If there is a birdwatchers' club in your nearest town they, too, will probably produce an annual report. These reports will contain a systematic list of dated occurrences and counts and (usually) some additional comments on weather, local population trends, local ringing results and rarity descriptions. These annual reports provide the closest, most detailed backcloth to your own observations and really are essential reading for any fact-collecting birdwatcher.

County ornithologies

By now most counties or provinces have also presented their ornithology in book or atlas form. Again these contain fully annotated lists of all the birds that have occurred within the region and narrative description of habitat, breeding population, migration and like subjects. Such a book gives you a historical appreciation of your local birds and, read with a map to hand, provides the quickest guide to the birds of an area unknown to you.

National journals

To add some national information to your local store, you should also read your country's journals of birdwatching. These appear periodically (usually monthly or quarterly) and offer regular news about both birds and birdwatchers, summarized results of national surveys, identification papers and so on.

Handbooks
Many classic bird books have become scarce and expensive, but libraries can often help you find them. Do consult – or dip in and out of – your national ornithological handbook. Handbooks are large works containing all the available information on birds, from field characters to distribution, breeding, feeding and social behaviour. Start with the latest, for it should include the recent advances in knowledge and will firmly set your local ornithology in a broader context, but do not ignore earlier works. Of the latter, those written in the late 19th century are particularly interesting, for they illustrate how far birdwatching has advanced – in a nutshell, from shotgun to binoculars.

◀ **The peregrine was the subject of a monograph by Derek Ratcliffe.**

Monographs
Another classic kind of bird book is the monograph, a volume devoted entirely to just one family, species or ornithological subject. There is no better example than the bird volumes in "The New Naturalist" series, published by Collins. Within them, you will find the fullest poss-

ible treatment of birds as different as fulmar and hawfinch or tits and sea-birds. Why not borrow several and understand how far-reaching bird study can be? In the same series, you can also find broader ecological texts. Of these, *The Natural History of The Highlands and Islands* (of Scotland) is a really inspiring book.

Narrative books
In your reading, you should also allow time for the vicarious enjoyment afforded by birdwatchers' and bird photographers' tales. Sadly this type of book is in decline but again your library should be able to resurrect titles by Sir Peter Scott, G. K. Yeates, and other authors of the less hurried postwar years. A particular favourite of mine is Robert Atkinson's *Island Going* but all such books are full of romping narrative *and* good practical advice.

Researching your local bird population
The first step is to obtain a copy of your regional ornithology and the last three annual bird reports that include records from your area. Read the book and scan the reports; then write a systematic list of the birds already known to exist in, or to visit, your area.

It makes sense to group your notes under the headings of breeding birds, winter visitors, regular migrants and vagrants; and to allow space for any marked habitat preferences, particularly local distributions and seasonal concentrations. In this way, you will have drawn the obvious ground rules for your own studies and marked the less obvious exceptions to them that will need special attention.

WHERE TO NEXT?

Do you want to specialize?

By now, you will have appreciated the main streams of birdwatching, in thought, study and practice. There are many options in these and I well remember how as a young observer I wandered among them. In the 1940s, egg collecting was not illegal and, like many of my generation, my first pursuits of birds were with that now forbidden aim in mind. Being a restless soul, however, I soon tired of looking for nests and, under the guidance of a gamekeeper, I began to see birds as a most beautiful part of the natural world and their migrations as their most exciting behaviour.

All through the 1950s, I was a besotted migration student and it was not until my 15th year as a birdwatcher that I realized how much more there was to study. This little piece of biography illustrates how easy it is to let birds rule your heart. There is nothing wrong with sheer enjoyment but I do wish that I had some of those years back.

So it will be worth your while to review your progress in birdwatching, after say eighteen months, and decide what you most want to do with your growing expertise. You may, of course, want to carry on dipping into a variety of birdwatching experiences. However, defining your special interests as early as possible could save you much later frustration.

The first step is to look at your birdwatching strengths and weaknesses. Is your sight more acute than most? Are your ears (sadly) less trustworthy? Do you enjoy the hunting most, or the gathering? Does some other personal interest or skill

– such as mountaineering, foreign travel, art, photography or sound recording – complement your birdwatching and so allow an unusual study? Such questions deserve answers, and from these you can decide what you most want to do. You might go on, for example, to crack the stiffest identification tests, or test theoretically a mass of facts (and so prove a concept), or perhaps slog round a mountainous study area for ten consecutive holidays.

The fieldwork behind these projects will be interesting and often exciting because birds, wherever you are watching them, are unpredictable. Writing up your findings may be a bit tough but stick with it. Firm results are very satisfying.

The best birdwatchers and ornithologists that I know are all identifiable by their union of highly developed skills with unique interests and studies, all deployed against a wide knowledge of natural history.

Sorting out your interests will give you a real chance of finding a lasting enthusiasm and also an opportunity to contribute something of value to natural science.

"Twitching"

The most obvious (and expensive) cult in birdwatching nowadays is the mere assembly of a long life-list – the total number of different species seen. To extend their lists constantly, more and more young observers spend their time plugging into the grapevine of bird news, harvesting it for the most delectable rarity, obtaining its map reference and

Twitching – an excellent opportunity for close-up
study of birdwatchers. The bird itself may prove
more elusive...!

instantly tearing off after it.

"Twitching", as this all-go, often no-sleep behaviour is called, can be tremendous fun but do try to resist total seduction by it. Over-indulgence leads to frustration and all too often when the bird absents itself, all that ensues is a meaning-less day of chat or distressing ornitho-political backbiting. Boring!

So try to take all the advice offered so far, and appreciate, for example, how the now common collared dove is just as exciting as the always rare bee-eater. In truth, the former's astonishingly explosive spread across Europe in this century is much more interesting than the latter's summer vagrancy. Try to bird-watch in the round, and you will find it more interesting.

Learning from other birdwatchers

The best short cut to the enjoyment of birds is to find a good ornithological friend. To find him you must seek out other birdwatchers, spot the expert among the just keen, and observe his skills and techniques. Then you simply ask for help.

The best way to get in touch with other birdwatchers is to join your local club or society. Its address and those of its main officers will be in the annual report (your lending library should have a copy). Don't be shy. Birdwatchers are a convivial lot and reserve a big welcome for new recruits. If you can show that you are also keen to take part, they will soon be asking for your help in local and even national cooperative surveys and studies.

Becoming a field ornithologist

Just when a keen birdwatcher becomes a field ornithologist is unclear. There is no exam to be passed and the change is marked more by a lasting increase in fact-gathering and summary than by passing success in rare bird hunting. To discover the full pleasures of field ornithology you will need to add some new skills to those you have already picked up in your early fieldwork. There are various places where you can go to see the skills of field ornithology in action. The rest of this section contains suggestions for three you can visit.

▼ Bramblings are one migratory species you may see at a bird observatory. They are winter visitors from Scandinavia.

Visiting a bird observatory

There is no more intensive ornithological experience – or better training – than that provided by a stay at a bird observatory.

These days most observatories apply broad, essentially scientific study techniques to all the birds in their area throughout the year. Increasingly they also monitor the fortunes of the rest of the local flora and fauna. So observatories present you with a marvellous chance to compare your knowledge with that of other observers, and to learn new or more advanced skills. Just a few days in the company of a helpful warden and other expert observers will teach you more than months of solitary watching.

Most bird observatories were set up principally to monitor migration, so they are generally located on coasts and islands. To get advice on which best accommodates the newcomer, you should again contact your local or national society officers. One of them will be bound to know the booking and travel arrangements and the best time to visit the observatory. Please note that, with few exceptions, bird observatories are devoted more to field study than to human comfort. So do not expect to be cossetted, and do read the joining instructions carefully.

Once at a bird observatory, try not to dash out on your own with eyes and binoculars all aglint for the first rarity. Stay close to the warden and initially pay as much attention to the study methods as to the birds themselves. During your visit you will be able to contribute to the counts of both grounded and flying birds, and help with concerted drives of birds into traps and nets. There will be a chance, too, to watch the handling of birds during ringing, and to closely examine plumage variation, and so on.

During the evenings, there will be a rollcall of the day's species, with discussions on types of migration or the variety of breeding birds and pointers, perhaps, on the identification of difficult species. As long as you stay awake, you will be learning, but do get some sleep. Dawn is always early and birds are at their busiest then. To get the most out of your stay, try to take notes not just on the birds but also on the study methods. These will give you numerous ideas for your own studies and future survey work.

Days at bird observatories are often long and full . . .

Scene 1 – Watching migrants at dawn.

Yellow wagtails

Scene 2 – Driving the Heligoland trap.

Scene 3 – Nesting peregrines can be seen at one observatory.

Scene 4 – Identifying a rare warbler before the sun goes down!

▼ If you can't get to an observatory, try to visit a ringing site to see ringers at work . . .

1. Taking birds from the net

4. Measuring the bird

5. Weighing the bird by spring balance

2. Carrying the birds in bags to the ringing hut

Pied flycatcher

6. Releasing the bird

Pliers

3. Ringing the bird

Visiting a ringing site

If you cannot get to a bird observatory, a visit to a site used by a group of ringers will give you a chance to observe the techniques of trapping and ringing.

Ringers are usually kept pretty busy, as their first duty is to release the birds quickly. So you may have to wait for answers to your questions. You can pick up a lot, though, by watching how they handle the birds and how they record the information they collect. Have a look, too, at the sites they pick for trapping and the species that turn up there. This will give you an idea of the population within a certain habitat and you may find one or two surprises.

Ringing groups work in a variety of habitats, often on inland sites. Local birdwatchers will know where your nearest group is based.

Visiting a bird museum

You will probably have been trailed past an exhibit of stuffed birds in your youth. Most of the specimens will have looked old (as they are, for the skins are often of birds shot 100 years ago), dusty, and – around the legs – brittle. Try to eradicate such memories and explore anew the greater treasures behind the museum's closed doors. Stored in the back rooms are thousands of skins, sorted geographically, and hundreds of reference books, shelved by subject.

To get behind the scenes in a museum can be a difficult exercise but do not be put off by the bureaucratic barriers. Insist that you are a genuine student and wish to increase your knowledge. Initially, I suggest that you keep your researches simple, for example the close examination of plumage colours and contours (feather sets) of a common species that you already know well, but later on, you could make them more complex. Only by spreading a range of skins along a museum bench can you see the wide range of sexual, seasonal and age differences that even a single species wears. Or you can examine the subtle changes in colour and patterns that mark geographical variation in birds and frequently merit the recognition of races or subspecies. These are subjects that relate to the taxonomy or classification of birds and to get a grasp of them, one day in a museum can be worth years of field study.

Lesser redpoll (upperside) Lesser redpoll (underside) Mealy redpoll Arctic redpoll

▲ **Museum skins, showing considerable variation between the two European races of redpoll – lesser and mealy – and their close cousin the Arctic redpoll.**

For information on observatories, ringing groups and museums contact your local library, local birdwatchers' club or get hold of a copy of Birdwatcher's Yearbook (see page 126).

Contributing to national records

So much happens in the world of birds every year that the ornithological records of Europe's nations will never be complete. The amateur can still carry out extremely useful studies. If you are worried about starting, just remember that all the leading observers of today had to begin somewhere. There's always something new to find.

The earlier sections in this book introduced you to some local and national study aims and methods. I hope that you will want to get involved in these but there are many other ways for you to contribute to your national ornithology.

My first published note was of a lesser yellowlegs in southern Scotland in the spring of 1950 (see the illustrations opposite). Then it was exceptional for an American wader to appear in that season, and the editor of *British Birds* (see page 127) considered the bird worthy of the national news. Nowadays the record would not merit full publication but there will always be others that do.

How you can contribute
You can best judge the types of record and study to which the amateur contributes from your own reading and the comments of a helpful expert.

In order of current popularity (but not necessarily scientific merit), amateurs contribute in four main areas. You can (1) submit rare bird records to your national review body, (2) offer your own perceptions of field characters (identification points) to the relevant national journal, (3) report on unusual behaviour, or (4) summarise significant results from your surveys or studies.

The last may range widely and can represent the most permanent and enjoyable products of your bird-watching. Working with others I have recently helped to redefine the seabird passage off eastern Britain. Right now I am bursting to investigate the winter feeding behaviour of the redpoll. No-one else has and it is just this sort of study that allows you to compete with the professional.

Writing up your results
The illustrations opposite show how two friends and I explored the sighting of the lesser yellowlegs and turned the observation into a published "note". Short "notes" are the best way to present a single observation on behaviour or identification.

Multiple observations of any kind may require a longer write-up, "Reports", for instance, deal systematically with such subjects as the bird life of a region (your local bird report, for example). "Papers" examine at length particular pieces of research and survey work.

Preparing the notes, reports and papers that will turn the raw data in your notebooks and logs into well written conclusions requires some dedication. Well directed efforts will be constructively criticised by ornithological editors. They will be happy to give advice, in the form of examples of writing construction, a list of other literary references, and so on.

To avoid disappointment, there are three golden rules. First make sure that you have something new or significantly different to contribute. Second, demonstrate that you have researched your subject fully. Third, never over-reach in deduction or conclusion – and be prepared to revise a conclusion if need be.

Discovery and observation ▶
While enjoying the common waders of Aberlady Bay on 13th May 1950, three young observers flush a "small greenshank" but are very puzzled by its yellow legs and square white rump. It is clearly a rarity but which? They watch the wader closely, making notes.

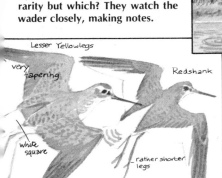

Lesser Yellowlegs

very tapering

Redshank

white square

rather shorter legs

fairly blunt

long legs, visible behind tail in flight

◀ *Noting unusual features*
The bird's size is difficult to judge, since its wings and legs are both proportionately longer than those of a redshank nearby. It also lacks the "round-shouldered" walk of that species and has a slower more buoyant flight. These points are stressed in the notes and help to identify the bird as a lesser yellowlegs from America!

Tracing the bird's origin ▶
In the early fifties, no-one fully understood how widely some American waders strayed in spring. Searching the weather records the observers find that there were strong westerly gales in late April. Perhaps the bird was windblown across the North Atlantic and Scotland at that time.

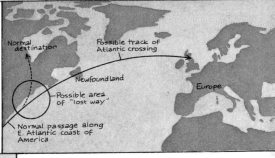

Normal destination

Possible track of Atlantic crossing

Newfoundland

Europe

Possible area of "lost way"

Normal passage along E. Atlantic coast of America

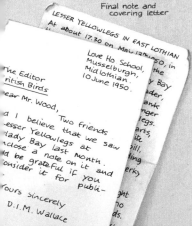

Final note and covering letter

LESSER YELLOWLEGS IN EAST LOTHIAN
At about 17.30 on May 13th 1950, in ...

Love Ho School, Musselburgh, Midlothian. 10 June 1950.

The Editor
ritish Birds

ear Mr. Wood,

a I believe that
esser Yellowlegs
lady Bay last month.
close a note on it and
ld be grateful if you
onsider it for publi-

ours sincerely
D.I.M. Wallace

◀ *Publication of a note*
On behalf of their school ornithological society, the observers write up a "note". This follows the style of other notes in *British Birds* and is submitted to the Editor. It is accepted by the national expert on the species and in December 1950 is published, becoming a piece of Britain's ornithological history. (See *British Birds*, Vol. 43, p.406).

Getting wider experience

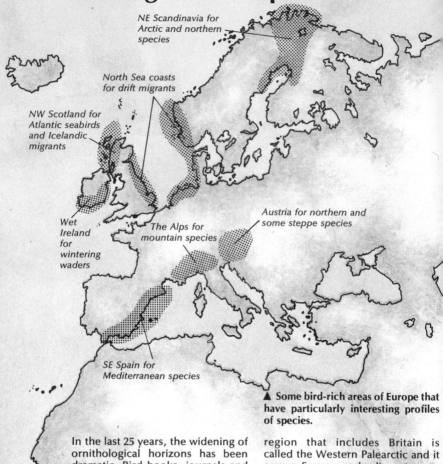

NE Scandinavia for Arctic and northern species

North Sea coasts for drift migrants

NW Scotland for Atlantic seabirds and Icelandic migrants

Wet Ireland for wintering waders

The Alps for mountain species

Austria for northern and some steppe species

SE Spain for Mediterranean species

▲ Some bird-rich areas of Europe that have particularly interesting profiles of species.

In the last 25 years, the widening of ornithological horizons has been dramatic. Bird books, journals and magazines have made more and more references to events abroad; packaged holidays and expeditions have sent birdwatchers all over the world; and natural scientists now look at broad faunal regions (large areas of the world which have breeding species in common) rather than just individual countries. The faunal region that includes Britain is called the Western Palearctic and it covers Europe and adjacent areas of Africa and the Middle East.

For me, the fact that Europe has a list of breeding species whose distribution may range from "widespread" to "local" is very exciting. Naturally, parts of Europe have habitats quite different from those found in the British Isles, so amongst your familiar species you will find

Red-footed falcon

White-winged
black terns

Great bustards

**Several East European species can be
seen on the steppe (grassland plains) of
Austria's eastern border.**

Barnacle geese feeding
on short grass

Greenland white-fronted geese
feeding in a damp, rushy hollow

**Large numbers of geese fly from their
Arctic breeding grounds to winter in
west Scotland.**

others that are new to you. For example, in Spanish maquis (sharp, hillside scrub), you may find wood-chat shrike and black-eared wheat-ear alongside the more familiar kestrel and stonechat.

I know of no more fascinating travel experience than to see the changes in passing countryside and to spot the birds that signpost the different habitats within the whole. By visiting the regions of Europe that have particularly interesting profiles of species, you will begin to under-stand the inter-relationships of your own birds more fully.

Take a close look at the distribution maps and habitat notes in your field guide and handbook before you select a route or a centre for overseas observations. In the mean-time, the map on page 116 will show you the explorations that have taught me most about the distribution of European birds. I have not yet been to Yugoslavia and Greece but expeditions there are worthwhile.

Getting a wider experience of birds will give you a fuller under-standing of their distribution, the habitat preferences of individual species and the overlaps in habitat selection that allow their com-munities to mix.

Looking at the different ranges of species within Europe

In Europe, the last of the Ice Ages retreated 10,000 years ago but its effects are still detectable.

By travelling along a SW/NE line in western Europe and a N/S one in eastern Europe, you can virtually roll back time and sense the shifts in range of Arctic, Continental, Temp-erate and Mediterranean species. A good example of such a feature is the so-called "chaffinch/brambling line" which runs across northern Scandinavia. South and west of it, the chaffinch (a Continental species) exploits most treed habitats and is resident in much of Europe. North of it only the brambling (a sub-Arctic species) is adapted to living in the few deciduous trees of the northern conifer forests but it stays only to breed, moving south in winter.

▼ Spain's hot, dry climate attracts Mediterranean species that can also be found in North Africa.

Hoopoe

Rufous bushchat

Bee-eater

Taking a break

Taking an occasional break from your usual birdwatching studies, however fascinating, is important. A day's expedition to a bird-rich area will provide some exciting moments and seeing new species in different habitats should set your mind thinking. Here, then, are a few ideas of places to go for some great birdwatching moments.

▲ Whooper swans on a misty morning.

Visiting a wildfowl refuge

There is no more inspiring sight than herds of wildfowl strewn across a wide sky or scattered through an ancient wetland. Happily, western Europe (and its Atlantic climate) offers many chances to see winter assemblies of ducks, geese and swans that have flown from breeding grounds as distant as Siberia.

In Britain, one of the most evocative – and certainly the most educational – places to watch wildfowl is at Slimbridge, the home of the Wildfowl Trust on the uppermost reach of the Severn Estuary. Slimbridge has both a tame wildfowl collection and hordes of wild birds. So if your head is turned by the gaggles of wild geese or the whistles of wigeon, this is the place for you.

Once you have used its excellent hides and double-checked your identification of wild birds against their tame cousins in the nearby collection, you will be well prepared to explore the many other winter wetlands of Britain and Ireland. Their list is long, for example, north Norfolk and the Wash, the Essex estuaries, Poole Harbour (excellent for grebes), and the Wexford Slobs. So your winter expeditions need never lack variety of species and scene.

Wandering through a southern woodland

Few wooded habitats in central and southern Europe have been left undisturbed, and finding one that has kept its ancestral flora and fauna is not easy. Birdwatching in an ancient wood is however a special experience worth a long journey.

In Britain and Ireland, the forests that sprang up after the Ice Age have been almost totally destroyed but there are a few isolated patches left. The best in terms of bird life is the New Forest and there in a long summer day you can still see strong glimmers of the diversity of species once common to all lowland England. In fact, a wander through its groves and across its heaths is the nearest to a truly European bird-watching experience that a British observer can have.

During your walk, look out particularly for birds of prey. Two scarce species may appear overhead at any time. They are the lithe hobby and the strange, wasp-eating honey buzzard. Among the gorse, watch out for the Dartford warbler, Britain's only resident among that normally migratory tribe.

Other pieces of broad-leaved forests are scattered around England and even those close to cities may support some surprising birds. The one that I know best is Epping Forest, near London, which is an excellent place for all three woodpeckers, the elusive hawfinch and – once to date – the mysterious short-toed treecreeper, widespread in Europe but with its true status over here a series of question marks. A glance at a map will soon reveal your nearest dense wood. Do go and enjoy it.

▼ The New Forest's heathlands and its oak, beech and pine woods harbour some interesting species.

Hobby

Buzzard

Yellowhammer

Dartford warbler

Exploring a reedmarsh

The last patches of ancient fenland and marsh are, like the old woods, widely scattered and still threatened. Luckily conservationists have recently given them much attention and some of these bird-rich communities are open to you and me. Huge reedbeds make for difficult birdwatching. So if you are to revel fully in it, take your time: a true case of waiting and seeing.

The most famous bird reserve in Britain is also the nation's most splendid marsh – Minsmere in Suffolk. To get into its magic hides, you must first join the RSPB (see page 126) and then wait patiently for an entry permit. I do advise you to do both, however, for Minsmere on a late spring or early summer day can be breathtaking. Below is my account of one short visit there.

▲ Bearded tits are totally adapted to living in reedbeds.

21 May 1972
An early morning at Minsmere

I didn't bother with sleep and drove straight from the end of the late film to East Bridge, arriving at 0345. It was still dark; so I moved on to Dunwich and drove slowly along the heath lanes. On the end one, I ran slap into not one but at least three nightjars – all glowing red eyes and winking white wing panels in my headlights – and I was smiling – before dawn – at such an unexpected gift.

It's always good to start with a surprise. I took a look from the sandcliff but the light was still poor. So I went back towards East Bridge, fancying a walk along the stream rather than the usual plod across the shingle strand. Every pause made on the overland lane produced several nightingales in full song. One was literally only a few feet from the car window and I could hear the growls

and grace notes as well as the pulsing crescendos. More magic!

Down at the bridge, the dawn was beginning to break and I struck out east. A heavy dew and Suffolk nettles combined to make my progress a soggy and stinging experience but it mattered little, as a drake garganey fluttered up, snipe drummed and sedge warblers chortled everywhere. My adrenalin continued to flow. Canada geese with young broods in the nearby ditch honked furiously at my passing but suddenly a much more exciting sound reached my ears. It was a continuous reeling and could only be coming from a grasshopper warbler or a much rarer Savi's warbler. The bird – or was it two? – lead me something of a stationary dance but, at last, patience paid off. It shuffled up a taller reed and a clear view showed that it was indeed a Savi's. Hardly believing my luck, I moved on with the sight of the morning's

121

Nightjar

Red-backed
Shrike

Canada Goose
family

Marsh
Harrier

Nightingale

Savi's
Warbler

Garganey

Terek
Sandpiper

Kentish
Plover

Temminck's
Stint

Broad-billed
Sandpiper

first marsh harrier and the calls of bittern and avocet spurring my legs.

Given the grapevine news, I wasn't surprised to find the public shorehide already tenanted and the nearest reserve hide obviously guarded. Indeed there was a distinct air of ornithological siege. Squeezing in amongst several friends, I soon learnt that they had the broad-billed sandpiper in view. Given the crush and tension, it was not until I borrowed a telescope that I was certain of it. Contrary to its book image, it was dashing about and feeding actively like its dunlin companions!

Of the main target – an almost mythical terek sandpiper – there was no sign, and after an hour I became restless. So I went back to the bridge, getting superb views of a bittern and the cock marsh harrier but not hearing the Savi's again.

Back at East Bridge I was treated to the astonishing sight of a snipe perched on a telegraph wire and I also took the opportunity to brush up on reed warblers. Since the last of their tribe that I had studied were paddyfield and Blyth's reed warbler in Baluchistan five weeks before, the comparison was most useful.

Snatching a traditional pork pie and apple snack on the way, I circled back to the cliff car park – picking up a beautiful cock red-backed shrike on the way – and moved along to the shore for a second stare at the Scrape. The besieging forces had grown and the latest news on the terek had been acquired from a tetchy warden. "Still here – but in a hidden pool!" A difficult time ensued and I soon gave up the hides for wandering along the coast, picking up six black-tailed godwits, a Kentish plover, a late pintail, and the usual terns, and just enjoying

◄ The author's illustration of some highlights in a morning's birdwatching at Minsmere in Suffolk.

the place itself.

At 0830 I went back into the hide near the sluice and pulled my concentration back together. A wandering stint was confirmed as a Temminck's, and hardly had it been noted when a voice yelled out "What's this?!" Bent double, I peered out and there, scampering about with classic gallop, was the terek sandpiper. I rushed out to spread the word but the fickle bird immediately returned to its sanctuary. So sadly many others were disappointed. Never mind, I had had a splendid morning's birds and could speed home quite untroubled!

Other ideas

The suggestions above have directed you to three great natural spectacles and described a visit to one of them. There are many other places to visit (some are listed on pages 124–125) and you will probably discover your own favourite spots.

Great birdwatching moments are not confined to bird reserves and observatories. It can be an exciting experience, for example, to watch the aerial floods of birds coming to a roost or passing along a hillside or headland, or to find newly-come migrants hiding in foggy coastal bushes after a night of east wind.

Sewage farms, incidentally, should not be forgotten, with their mass of chattering starlings, pied wagtails and gulls by the hundred, and always the possibility of an unusual wader.

If it is the odd rarity that beckons you, then a long trip to Fair Isle or Scilly will provide the best odds on such. There you will find the north and south-west poles of British ornithology, hordes of the keenest observers and more uncommon birds than anywhere else in Europe!

THE BIRDWATCHER'S ROUND

Reserves and bird observatories

In spite of the marked habitat losses of the last two centuries, there are happily many bird haunts that have been saved and a growing few that have been created. There follows a selection of those that present the most exciting ornithological pageants. Fuller lists have been published in *Birdwatcher's Yearbook* and *Where to Watch Birds*, both listed on pages 126–127.

SCOTLAND

Sands of Forvie and Ythan Estuary (NCC), Grampian. Take A975 to Newburgh, north of Aberdeen; park in spaces provided and take note of seasonal changes of access. Habitats range from huge sand dunes to long muddy estuary; birds include largest British colony of eiders, four species of terns and a winter circus of grey geese.

Loch Garten (RSPB) and Loch an Eilean (NCC); Highlands. Take side roads, respectively north-east and south-east of Aviemore; park in spaces provided and keep to paths or nature trail. Closely adjacent areas providing access to heart of Scotland's most ancient forests; birds include the famous ospreys, the majestic capercaillie, crossbill and crested tit. Access to nearby Cairngorm Mountains by ski lift.

Fair Isle, Shetland. To visit, contact the Warden, Fair Isle Bird Observatory, By Lerwick, Shetland. Large, encliffed, oceanic island; breeding birds include skuas, twite and endemic Fair Isle wren; migrants include more rarities than anywhere else in Europe. A *locus classicus* for all keen birdwatchers.

WALES

Cors Tregaron (NCC), Dyfed. Approach by A485 and B4343 north of Tregaron; park carefully and do not stray from signed path; best watching is of "wait and see" type. Example of raised peat bog, surrounded by upland farms and wooded hillsides; birds include wintering red kites, buzzards, grasshopper warblers and lesser redpolls.

Lake Vyrnwy (RSPB), Powys. Encircled by B4393; park carefully and keep to nature trail. Upland lake surrounded by woods; breeding birds range from goosander to redstart and pied flycatcher.

Bardsey Island, off Gwynedd. To visit the observatory, contact the Booking Secretary, 21a Gestridge Road, Kingsteignton, Newton Abbot, Devon (0626) 68580. 450 acre island, supporting breeding Manx shearwaters, storm petrels and choughs, and often receiving large falls of night migrants; rarities always of special interest.

ENGLAND

Bempton Cliffs (RSPB), Yorkshire. Approach along B1255 from Bridlington, turning north-west in Flamborough and north at Bempton; park at end of lane and tread carefully along cliff edge. Habitat essentially the north face of Britain's eastern cape, supporting the only mainland colony of gannets, thousands of auks and hundreds of thousands of kittiwakes.

Blakeney Point, Cley and Salthouse (National Trust and Norfolk Naturalists' Trust), Norfolk. Skirted by A149, in places winding and narrow, so drive carefully and park only in spaces provided. Habitats range from sand and shingle to saltings and reedbeds and are probably the most searched of any in Britain; local list contains over 300 species, with shore larks, snow buntings and brent geese in winter, a chance of any marsh species in summer and regular falls of many migrants in spring and autumn. Together with the woods of Wells-next-the-sea, these are the best migrant haunts in England and excellent training grounds for young observers.

Stodmarsh (NCC), Kent. Approach by A257 from Canterbury, then by side road to Stodmarsh; park carefully and walk north to marsh wall. Habitat essentially a huge freshwater marsh, extended by winter flooding; birds include resident Cetti's warbler, winter wildfowl and summer visitors to reedbed, notably sedge, reed and grasshopper warblers. Many garganey appear in spring.

Poole Harbour and surround, Dorset. Approach by various routes. Harbour best in winter, with black-tailed godwits, small grebes and saw-billed ducks nowhere more obvious in England. Relict heaths subject to strict conservation and restricted access but still give good chance of stonechat and even Dartford warbler on reserve edges. Excellent area for birdwatching holiday in any season.

Martin Mere (Wildfowl Trust), Lancashire. Watch for signs on A59 at Burscough Bridge and A565 at Mere Brow; park as indicated and enjoy wide range of amenities and spectacle, which now rival those at Slimbridge. Birds include up to 18,000 pink-footed geese, hen harriers and

merlin in winter and an excellent variety of waders all year.

Dungeness (RSPB), Kent. Approach through Lydd, aiming at the nuclear power stations, inland of which is the bird observatory (easternmost cottage within shingle "moat") and its trapping area. To the north lie various gravel pits, some managed as reserves. Beware wandering into shelling range. Habitat unique, with shifting shingle base and huge patches of gorse, brambles and stunted trees, often flooded. Birds include lowest level breeding wheatears in Britain, occasional floods of migrants and fascinating passage of seabirds, notably little gull and marsh terns. The best station to observe modern bird-trapping techniques.

IRELAND

Wexford Wildfowl Reserve (IWC), Co. Wexford. Approach from Wexford, with side roads to either North or South Slob. Habitat essentially wet, flat farmland surrounding natural inlet with Sandy Island. Birds include roseate tern in summer and thousands of white-fronted geese in winter, the latter picking up fellow travellers as rare as snow goose and the wild small races of Canada goose.

Cape Clear, Co. Cork. To visit the observatory, contact the Booking Secretary, 46 The Glen, Boden Park, Dublin 14. Large, rocky, rolling island off one of Ireland's southwestern capes; birds include breeding chough and black guillemot and many vagrants, particularly transatlantic ones, but main study is of oceanic passages in July and August, annually featuring great and Cory's shearwaters.

National societies

Your choice of national society membership will depend on your interests but all of the following deserve at least your occasional support.

British Trust for Ornithology (BTO), Beech Grove, Station Road, Tring, Herts HP23 5NR. Tel: (044-282) 3461. Harnesses the fieldwork of amateurs for conservation-oriented studies organised by itself and other national organisations; also administers the national ringing scheme and most of the major bird observatories. Publishes *BTO News* and quarterly journal *Bird Study*, plus highly informative guides on many subjects, ranging from taxonomy to migration periods.

Field Studies Council (FSC), Preston Montford, Montford Bridge, Shrewsbury, Shropshire SY4 1HW. Tel: (0743) 850674. Aims to improve appreciation of natural world for any student, organising short courses on many natural history subjects. Publishes *Field Studies*.

Irish Wildbird Conservancy (IWC), c/o Royal Irish Academy, 19 Dawson Street, Dublin 2, Ireland. Coordinates and leads all birdwatching studies in Ireland, liaising with government on conservation. Publishes *IWC News* and *Irish Birds*, plus informative booklets.

Royal Society for the Protection of Birds (RSPB), The Lodge, Sandy, Bedfordshire SG19 2DL. Tel: (0767) 80551. Manfully protects Britain's bird habitats and their common and uncommon inhabitants; enthuses and educates over 340,000 members and opinion leaders; reacts to all current and future threats to birds. Publishes *Birds*, special reports, and wide range of birdwatching aids; makes excellent films.

World Wildlife Fund (WWF), Panda House, 11–13 Ockford Road, Godalming, Surrey GU7 1QU. Puts together international awareness of threats to natural world and endangered species, and generates widespread support for corrective measures, including cash grants for reserves. Publishes *World Wildlife News* and *World Wildlife Yearbook*.

Young Ornithologists' Club (YOC). Address as RSPB. Enthuses and guides over 111,000 birdwatchers under 18, providing training and study opportunities. Publishes *Bird Life*.

Books and journals

Here is a short list of books. It includes those mentioned in the preceding text and others that you can seek out in bookshops or libraries. Libraries should be able to find out-of-print titles.

INTRODUCTIONS TO
BIRDWATCHING
Discover Birds Ian Wallace (Whizzard Press/André Deutsch 1979). Generally acknowledged as the most evocative introduction published in recent years. **Birdwatcher's Yearbook 1981** (published annually since then). John E. Pemberton (Buckingham Press 1980). Packed with useful facts, references and details of reserves, observatories, local clubs and national societies; shortens the beginner's search to all sorts of things ornithological.

FIELD GUIDES

Usborne Guide to Birds of Britain & Europe Rob Hume (Usborne 1981). Well-illustrated guide to a selection of common species.

The Mitchell Beazley Birdwatcher's Pocket Guide Peter Hayman (Mitchell Beazley 1979). Slim, wallet-sized guide to common and regular species.

A Field Guide to the Birds of Britain and Europe R. Peterson, G. Mountfort and P. A. D. Hollom (Collins 1954, revised edition 1982). Classic field guide, with the best illustrations and text of all – but less comprehensive than the next title.

The Birds of Britain and Europe with North Africa and the Middle East H. Heinzel, R. Fitter and J. Parslow (Collins 1972). The best alternative to "Peterson" with a useful series of maps.

SCIENTIFIC HANDBOOKS

The Handbook of British Birds H. F. Witherby, F. C. R. Jourdain, N. F. Ticehurst and B. W. Tucker (Witherby 1938). The most influential handbook ever published and still the best reference to all but rare birds.

The Popular Handbook of British Birds P. A. D. Hollom (Witherby 1952). Condensed version of above five-volume work.

DISTRIBUTION OF BRITISH BIRDS

The Atlas of Breeding Birds in Britain and Ireland J. T. R. Sharrock (T. & A. D. Poyser for BTO/IWC 1976). Maps and discusses the breeding distribution and population trends of all British and Irish breeding birds; best yet example of how birdwatching becomes field ornithology.

LIST OF BIRDWATCHING SITES

Where to Watch Birds John Gooders (André Deutsch 1967, Pan 1977). Full details of approach route to and birds within Britain's major birdwatching stations.

GOOD READS

Seventy years of birdwatching H. G. Alexander (T. & A. D. Poyser 1974). Fascinating echoes of 20th century field ornithology across the world.

Island Going R. Atkinson (Collins 1949). Enjoyable account of seaborne expeditions after seabirds.

Natural History in the Highlands and Islands (of Scotland) Frank Fraser Darling (Collins 1949). Inspiring survey of the fauna and flora of an ancient region, with full discussion of Man's assault upon it.

Bill Oddie's Little Black Bird Book W. E. Oddie (Eyre Methuen 1980). Hilarious, bubble-bursting review of modern birdwatching – and particularly birdwatchers' behaviour.

Bird Haunts in Northern Britain G. K. Yeates (Faber and Faber 1948). Excellent example of bird photographer's work and travels in post-war period.

Birdwatching in the Seventies Ian Wallace (Macmillan 1981). Summarises major bird and birdwatching events in each season of the 1970s.

PERIODIC JOURNALS

Birds RSPB members' quarterly magazine. Lavishly illustrated, topical news of birds and their protection.

British Birds Monthly by annual subscription (enquiries to: BB Circulation, Fountains, Park Lane, Blunham, Bedford MK44 3NJ). Central, topical voice of British birdwatching and field ornithology, with best content balance of all journals.

THE USBORNE NATURALIST'S CODE

U se your countryside well. Protect all natural habitats, avoid causing any damage, and guard against all risk of fire.

S ave plant species from destruction. Learn which species are rare or protected by law. If you find a rare species, leave it alone and don't gossip about it. Report the sighting to the Nature Conservancy Council.

Never uproot whole plants, avoid trampling vegetation or picking flowers – many species have become rare through over-picking. Restrict your plant recording to photographs, notes and drawings.

B eware of permanently disrupting animals' homes or habitats. If you lift up seaweed, a stone, or a log, or if you move a bird's nest or the vegetation covering a burrow entrance, try and replace it the way it was.

Litter can kill and maim animals – take it all home.

O bserve the codes of conduct for nature photographers, bird-watchers, botanists and entomologists. These can be obtained from libraries and museums and from individual natural history clubs and societies.

R espect the rights of landowners, farmers and others who live and work in the country. Fasten all gates and keep to pathways across farmland. Where there are no paths, keep to the edge of the field.

N ever disturb wild animals. If your presence is causing alarm, move away quietly. Keep dogs under complete control at all times.

E nable wild animals to survive. Restrict your animal collecting to shells, bones, feathers and skulls picked up off the ground. Learn which species of animal are rare and protected by law.

WATCHING
WILDLIFE

INTRODUCTION

This section provides the basics of where, when, and how to watch animals in the wild. It shows how, with a little effort, you can experience the natural world at first hand, by relearning how to detect and observe mammals, birds, reptiles, amphibians, and small invertebrates, such as insects and spiders. The skills that were second nature to our ancestors can be reawakened, and used to open up a fascinating new world that begins right on your own doorstep.

The first few chapters of this section describe the techniques of locating the animals, then tracking or attracting them, and getting in close to watch them. They explain what you should take with you, and why, and provide a wealth of practical information on observing, understanding, photographing and recording what you see. Projects throughout this section will challenge your skills and shed new light on the hidden worlds around us.

Later chapters in this section describe the habits and habitats of many of the animals you are likely to see, with further tips on how best to observe them.

Once the basics of fieldcraft have been mastered, more detailed field guides and handbooks will be useful to you; a brief selection is listed on page 189. If you wish to develop your skills further, you can seek help and advice from members of the various wildlife societies and clubs, also listed on page 189.

The naturalist's code

The "golden rule" of watching wildlife is that the animal's welfare comes first. Anyone can blunder about and perhaps catch a fleeting glimpse of a fleeing animal but it takes skill, understanding and patience to observe without being detected. It takes practice, but the rewards are huge. Good fieldcraft might well be repaid by the sight of fox cubs wrestling by moonlight, by the "plop" of a water vole diving into a stream, or by the sight and sound of a red deer stag bellowing his challenge to all comers.

▼ A well-positioned observer is rewarded for his skill and patience as the fox closes in.

A battle of wits

All animals have a powerful instinct for survival. Their senses are ever alert to danger and while some rely on camouflage to protect them, others rely on speed to make their escape. Their tolerance of man, however, is very variable and this makes some species much easier to observe than others.

Many birds and insects are quite easy to approach and observe. Mammals are by far the most difficult – but also the most rewarding. It is an exciting challenge to pit your wits and knowledge against an animal's survival instinct and acute senses, and the main ingredients for success are stealth, cunning, patience and preparation – including a well-thought-out plan. While our eyesight and hearing are as good as those of some animals, they come a poor second to those of many more. As for our sense of smell, it barely exists. We cannot even imagine its sensitivity in animals like the fox or deer. (Who are we to say the fox is a smelly animal? We can smell him at thirty yards, but he can smell us at half a mile or more!)

Generations ago we lost the need to use our senses instinctively but with a little practice we can retune them to life in the wild, even though we can never hope to match those of the animals we seek.

Moving through woodland
Movement will betray your presence to everything from a butterfly to a badger, so learning how to remain still is as important as learning how to move with the minimum of noise. One of the best ways to see wildlife is to choose a likely spot in a wood and then sit perfectly still, with your back against a tree (see below). After a while the animals will emerge and go about their normal business; you will see far more than on a dozen

▼ **By keeping quiet and still this observer has become "part of the background" and will be ignored by the woodland wildlife until she stands up or makes a careless movement.**

Treecreeper

Great spotted woodpecker

Nuthatch

Roe deer

Squirrel

Woodpigeons

Rabbits

▲ When out walking, keep a sharp lookout for woodpigeons, jays or crows and avoid them if possible. All are superb sentries, and woodpigeons in particular will "explode" from their tree with a tremendous din at your approach – sending every other animal straight into hiding.

walks through the same area.

When you *do* walk, keep to damp grass, avoiding dry leaves and twigs. The crack of a dry twig is about the quickest way known of sending everything into hiding. If you use a path regularly, make a habit of removing such tell-tales – especially near a badger sett or bird's nest. To walk silently on leaves for short distances, wear soft shoes and at each step gently move your foot from side to side to clear the leaves out of the way. If you have to walk through leaves for a longer distance it is better to slide the feet – making a soft continuous noise rather than a loud intermittent one. Remember that damp vegetation is always less noisy than dry, so walks after rain, or with morning dew still on the ground, are often the most fruitful.

Riverbank and marsh

Always try to "read" the landscape and plan your route for concealment and quietness. On the riverbank try to walk on grass or sand, avoiding noisy shingle and clinking stones. If you need to climb the bank, do so where you can climb smoothly and safely, without dislodging an avalanche of earth, and if possible where bushes will give cover as you reach the top.

When moving through reeds, wait for them to sway in the breeze and move with them, stopping again as each gust dies away. The same applies in any long vegetation. If you fit your own movements to any natural rhythms you will be rather less conspicuous.

In open country

When you are stalking animals in open country, wind direction takes on even greater importance. Check constantly and change your route as often as necessary to keep you down-wind of the animals. Move steadily, stopping frequently to look and listen, and above all do not talk. Try to keep your subject in sight and learn from its reactions. If startled it will flee; if just suspicious it will remain quite still until satisfied that it was a "false alarm". If possible, stalk animals when they are feeding or otherwise engaged, but remain alert and "freeze" the second an animal looks in your direction. Move again when it has resumed its activities – and when nearby animals have ceased to show concern.

The art of concealment

Camouflage is a very effective means of concealment that uses colour, pattern and texture to break up the tell-tale outline of an animal's body and help it blend in with its natural background. It can take many forms, from the elaborate disguises of many insects to the sand-speckled colouring of a flatfish and the delicately marked coat of a young fawn that merges so well with the light-dappled floor of the forest (see opposite). Some animals have this protection only when young and vulnerable; others, like the remarkable bittern of our reedbeds, are protected in adult life. Some creatures, like the Arctic fox, the stoat and the ptarmigan, change their colouring according to the season; but the picture of the stoat opposite shows what happens when this change is not quite fast enough!

▲ Concealed by his drab clothing, his boulder-strewn position, and by the dark hillside behind him, this naturalist watches deer feeding on the slopes below. Only the sun glinting on his binoculars, or an unlucky shift in wind direction, is likely to cause him any problem.

▲ Full of enthusiasm but doomed to disappointment, talkative walkers stride over the brow of a hill. The local wildlife will have taken cover long before they arrive. The colourful jacket, excellent in bad weather or an emergency, would be better carried in the back-pack until needed.

By studying animal camouflage we too can learn the art of concealment. The first principle, however, is to remain still – for any movement will destroy the effectiveness of even the best camouflage.

Wear subdued colours that blend with the landscape. Dull browns and greens are good, but better still is the irregular disruptive patterning used on military camouflage jackets. This breaks up the symmetrical outline of the figure. The ·giveaway human outline can also be disguised against natural shapes. By sitting crouched among boulders on a hillside you become part of the outcrop; by standing with your back to a tree you again break up your shape. A hat or anorak hood will hide a shiny forehead and for very wary subjects the face can be darkened with smears of earth or be covered by a veil of dark netting. (Even for animals one of the biggest problems is to hide the glint of the eye.) But remember that none of this will work if you wear loose wellingtons that make a slapping sound, or if you have loose change jangling in your pocket.

Use natural cover at every opportunity but don't be tempted to fix leaves and twigs to your clothes. They rustle and shake at every slight movement and will frighten away every creature within earshot.

Keeping your head down

Remember that nothing will put an animal to flight faster than the sudden appearance of a human silhouette on the skyline. Keep below the brow of a hill; always look under, through, or round a hedge rather than over the top; and bear in mind that most of the animals you seek see the world virtually from ground level – it is *their* skyline you must beware of. If you have to crawl along the ground to get closer to your subject, use every bit of natural cover. Even the shallowest depression in the ground will completely hide you from an animal whose eye is only a few inches above the ground; nevertheless be very careful when you raise your head.

Breaking cover

Sometimes it is necessary to leave your cover but you can reduce the impact of your silhouette if you keep some cover, a hillside or wood, behind you. Always look carefully before stepping out of cover and never walk straight through a gateway or a gap in a hedge. Instead, peer round the edge first.

Lessons from nature

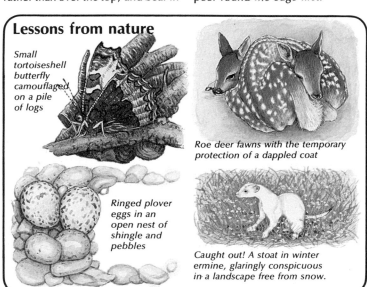

Small tortoiseshell butterfly camouflaged on a pile of logs

Roe deer fawns with the temporary protection of a dappled coat

Ringed plover eggs in an open nest of shingle and pebbles

Caught out! A stoat in winter ermine, glaringly conspicuous in a landscape free from snow.

Reading the signs

One of the most satisfying of all fieldcraft skills is the ability to read the subtle signs left by birds, insects and mammals as they go about their everyday lives. To the novice these signs are often very difficult to see but with practice they can be recognized quite readily and can add a new dimension to watching animals.

The most obvious signs are the tracks left by ground-dwelling animals and these are most clearly visible when made in a thin layer of fresh snow, in damp sand, or in soft, slightly muddy, ground. The best way to learn the various footmarks is to make careful drawings, to scale, each time you find one. You can also make casts of animal tracks using plaster of Paris poured into a retaining ring of card or metal pressed into the earth around the print. At some point you may even have the good fortune to come across the tell-tale marks of some natural drama: the tiny footprints of a mouse ending abruptly in disturbed snow showing the marks of an owl's feathers, or the scattered remains of a vole's nest left by a marauding fox.

But there is much more to the silent "language" of signs than just footprints. Vegetation of all types, from turnips to hazelnuts, pine cones to dandelions, may carry the marks of feeding animals – each one leaving its characteristic "signature" in the shape of the teeth marks, the part of the plant taken, the debris left behind, and the method of attack. Many animals and birds have favourite feeding places which may be littered with nut shells or splintered cones; birds in particular commonly wedge nuts or cones into bark crevices in order to peck at them, and again each species leaves

Bird pellet analysis

Measure the size of the pellet and note its shape. Then soak it and gently separate and identify the contents.

Common gull ▶
Up to 8cm long and 2cm in diameter. Variable content: fish bones, plant fibre and husks, insect remains.

◀ Sparrowhawk
Between 2 and 4cm long, about 1.5cm in diameter. Very firm and compact; made up mainly of mammal fur and small feathers.

its own "signature".

As animals eat, so they must get rid of bodily waste, and animal droppings can provide a fascinating source of information on what the resident animals have been eating. A great many birds pass only fluid waste in their droppings and retain the hard parts of ther diet (bits of shell, bones, insect wing-cases, grit and so on) which are then regurgitated from the crop in the form of a compact little bundle, or pellet (see above). These can be collected and broken open to reveal what the owl, or gull, or rook has been feeding on.

Once you become accustomed to tracks, feeding signs, territorial boundary marks and so on you will find yourself more and more adept at locating various animals' favourite routes and will therefore be able to track them more easily.

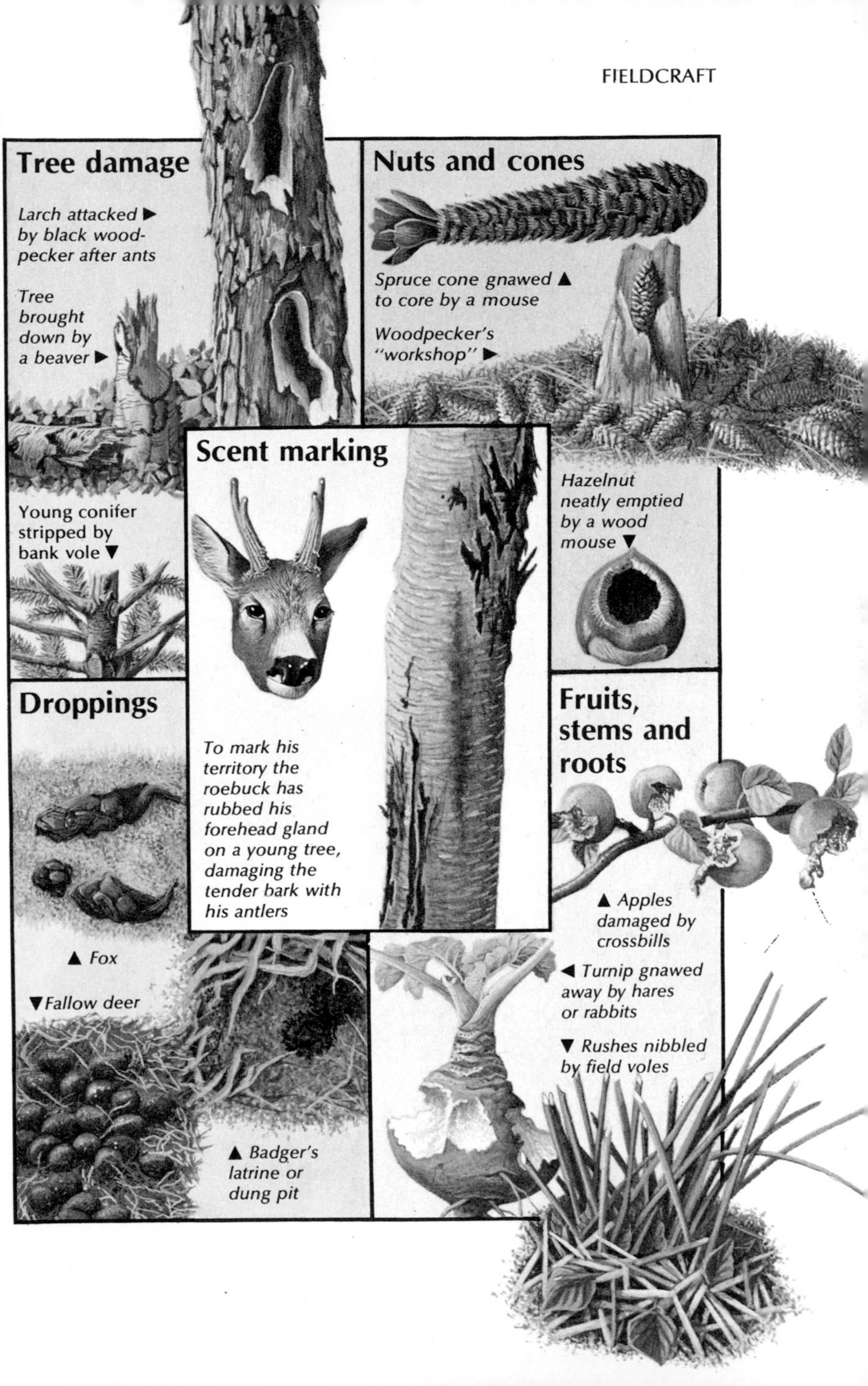

Tree damage

*Larch attacked ▶
by black wood-
pecker after ants*

*Tree
brought
down by
a beaver ▶*

*Young conifer
stripped by
bank vole ▼*

Nuts and cones

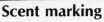

*Spruce cone gnawed ▲
to core by a mouse*

*Woodpecker's
"workshop" ▶*

*Hazelnut
neatly emptied
by a wood
mouse ▼*

Scent marking

*To mark his
territory the
roebuck has
rubbed his
forehead gland
on a young tree,
damaging the
tender bark with
his antlers*

Droppings

▲ Fox

▼Fallow deer

*▲ Badger's
latrine or
dung pit*

Fruits, stems and roots

*▲ Apples
damaged by
crossbills*

*◀ Turnip gnawed
away by hares
or rabbits*

*▼ Rushes nibbled
by field voles*

Getting in close

Once you are familiar with the basic ideas of camouflage, and using cover to disguise your movements, you can get down to the exciting business of getting in close to your subject. And that is when every trick of fieldcraft will be important. But don't be discouraged if insects fly off, or if rabbits bolt down their holes while you are still some way off. It takes time and practice to develop really good fieldcraft.

Try to remember always that while we watch animals for pleasure, animals watch each other (and man in particular) for far more serious reasons. Any large and unfamiliar shape, any strange sound, and especially any "foreign" scent, spells *Danger!* to a wild animal. This does not always mean, however, that the animal will bolt. Sometimes animals can be right under your feet, but so well concealed that you may not spot them. Learn to expect the unexpected – you may be surprised by what turns up!

For example, last summer I was filming in Jersey and had spent almost a whole day, very hot and very frustrated, looking for green lizards. Not one was to be seen. I contented myself filming some wild flowers and was walking back across the sand between thick tussocks of grass, when a metallic scraping sound caught my attention. At my feet was an old beer can. Two tiny eyes peered from the "keyhole" opening and my suspicions were soon confirmed by the flickering of a forked tongue and the flash of brilliant green scales. After a pause a beautiful green lizard the length of my foot emerged into the sunshine, blinked for a moment or two, and then scurried off, just like some

brilliantly-jewelled mechanical toy.

Normally, of course, you will have to use all the skills of fieldcraft to get so close to an animal. The following hints and tips may be of use.

Green lizard (male)

▲ **Many animals can squeeze through surprisingly small openings.**

Using an ash bag

A wet finger held aloft, or a light piece of grass tossed in the air, might tell you the wind direction when a gentle breeze is blowing, but even the lightest movement of air will carry your scent far and wide. So how are you to plan your stalk when you can't feel any wind?

The answer is to make an ash bag: a simple cotton bag, closed by a draw-string and filled with fine wood ash. To test the wind just flick the bag with a finger. The puff of ash will drift in the air and reveal even the slightest movement. The trick was devised many years ago by hunters in Africa: today we can put it to more peaceful purposes.

The benefits of snowfall

A thin, even, fall of snow is a great bonus to the wildlife watcher. Get out into the country near your home just as soon as possible and locate

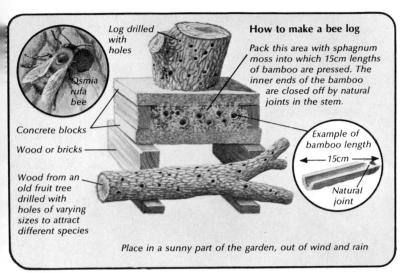

How to make a bee log

Log drilled with holes

Osmia rufa bee

Pack this area with sphagnum moss into which 15cm lengths of bamboo are pressed. The inner ends of the bamboo are closed off by natural joints in the stem.

Concrete blocks

Wood or bricks

Wood from an old fruit tree drilled with holes of varying sizes to attract different species

Example of bamboo length

◄— 15cm —►

Natural joint

Place in a sunny part of the garden, out of wind and rain

and identify as many animal tracks as you can. Make notes of where the trails cross the roads, where they pass through gates or gaps in hedges, and note where any animal has stopped to investigate something or to leave a scent mark.

All this information can be plotted on a sketch map, perhaps using colours for the different animals. Then, when the snow has gone, you will know just where to look for the tracks and very often you will also know exactly where the nest or burrow is so you will have ample time to plan a good observation position before the breeding season starts.

Make practice a habit
"Practice" sounds too much like homework, so make a game of it. If you are in a park, or out for a walk, try setting yourself puzzles. Pick a spot at the far side of a small valley, or across the local park or playing field. If there are feeding birds, or squirrels, between you and the target, so much the better. Then plan a route to the target using every scrap of available cover, assuming first that the wind is from your left, then from your right, from in front and from behind you. Whenever there is time, actually do the stalk – seeing how close to the birds or squirrels you can get before they scatter.

Attracting wildlife to you
One way of ensuring that you get close to an animal is to attract it to you in some way, either by baiting (see pages 152–3) or, as shown above, by providing it with suitable materials for making a home. A selection of ready-made nesting sites in a "bee log" will encourage solitary bees and wasps to nest in your garden, where you can then watch them.

Knowing when to leave

▼ Red deer stag roaring in rut
with unconcerned hinds
grazing nearby.

Although getting in close will be one of your main objectives, the true naturalist is always aware of the fact that he is an intruder and that his presence can have a marked effect on the behaviour of many animals. Learn to recognize the warning signs so that by knowing when to withdraw you will avoid doing any harm to the wildlife you wish to study.

In some situations (luckily not many) such knowledge may save you being on the receiving end of a sharp reminder of what is, and what is not, good fieldcraft. For example, it should go without saying that you never put your hand down a burrow unless you know for sure that it is unoccupied. Ignore that rule and you are asking to get your fingers badly bitten, stung or pecked (puffins make burrows too!)

Season of aggression

The ritualized combat of red deer in rut can be a spectacular sight but at the height of the autumn rutting (breeding) season the stags can be very unpredictable. More than one person has been charged after approaching too close – presumably having been taken as a potential rival by a stag vigorously defending his leadership of a herd of hinds. The alarm signal is a series of sharp barks, while suspicion is shown by the stag holding his head high while raising and lowering the forelegs in a slow, stiff, "high-stepping" motion.

Some of our larger birds can also be dangerous if approached on the nest. Swans and geese in particular can deliver a fierce attack so it is always wise to drop back if a sitting bird shows signs of agitation. It is also illegal to "wilfully disturb" most species of birds, so *never* approach a nest except in the company of an experienced, authorized bird-watcher.

◄ **Alpine marmot sitting upright in sentry posture with others feeding nearby.**

Social warnings

Many of the social mammals, and also many birds, post "sentries" while the majority are feeding. The European marmot is a typical example: a shrill whistle from a lookout will send the entire colony underground in a flash and even the Alpine chamois will react to the marmot's alarm signal.

The rabbit has a dual alarm system. An individual sensing danger will beat its hind feet on the ground to alert the others; the signal is reinforced by the flashing of the white tail as the rabbit runs for cover.

◄ **Toad inflated to put off attack by grass snake.**

Desperate measures

Extreme agitation can produce very unusual and apparently bizarre behaviour in some animals. Toads will react to threat by arching the back and throwing up the head, often inflating the body in an attempt to discourage the attacker. If handled roughly, the grass snake goes one better, twisting onto its back and lying quite still with its mouth agape in imitation of death.

Nesting birds in particular have a number of marked behaviour patterns indicating distress and these must be heeded *immediately*. If a parent bird is prevented from getting back to the nest it may become so distraught that it abandons the nest entirely – with the loss of the eggs or nestlings. Agitation may be shown by the bird darting back and forth with high-pitched cries or by more elaborate behaviour. A bird that remains nearby, continually preening itself, while you are watching the nest, is becoming increasingly agitated and you should withdraw immediately. More elabo-

Plover's broken ► wing trick.

rate still is the ploy used by a number of ground-nesting birds. The ptarmigan will defend its nest bravely and even if a chick is seized the parent will not flee but will beat the ground and feign a wing-injury in an effort to lure the attacker away to an apparently "easy" victim. The shore-nesting ringed plover is another superb exponent of the "broken wing" trick.

The fact that an animal is alarmed does not automatically mean an end to the day's watching; a temporary withdrawal may be all that is required. Recognizing the signs that an animal knows you are there may perhaps enable you to keep it in view all afternoon instead of seeing it take fright and disappear.

OBSERVING AND RECORDING
What to carry

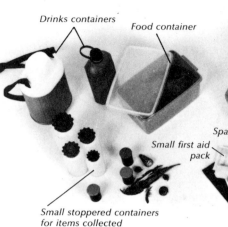

Conspicuous waterproof outer clothing in case you want to be seen, e.g. in hill country

Spare clothing

Drinks containers

Food container

Spare film

Camera

Small first aid pack

Ordnance Survey map in map case

Compass

Small stoppered containers for items collected

Torch with red filter

Battery

Whistle

Hand lens (×10)

Pocket knife

The most valuable aid for the wildlife watcher is a good pair of binoculars. A wide range of choice is available and nowadays a good pair need not cost a fortune. When buying, test as many different pairs as possible – always stepping outside the shop to test them in daylight and over a range of distances.

The magnifying power and light-gathering ability of binoculars are given by numbers: 8×40, 7×50, 6×30 and so on. The first number is the magnification; the second is the diameter, in millimetres, of the objective lens and this governs the light-gathering capacity. To find the diameter of the exit pupil (the eyepiece lens) you divide the large number by the smaller. The exit diameter of a 6×30 is therefore 5mm. Anything above 4mm will be adequate for wildlife-watching.

Higher magnifications may sound attractive but they are difficult to

Notebook and pencils

Pouched belt for travelling light

keep steady. For wildlife watching, ×7 or ×8 magnification, coupled with good light-gathering, gives the best results, so you could try 8×40 or 7×50, whichever suits your eyesight. Generally, the higher the magnification, the smaller is the angle of view although some binoculars are described as "wide-angle". Locating an animal with binoculars is not as easy as with the naked eye so a wide angle of view is very useful.

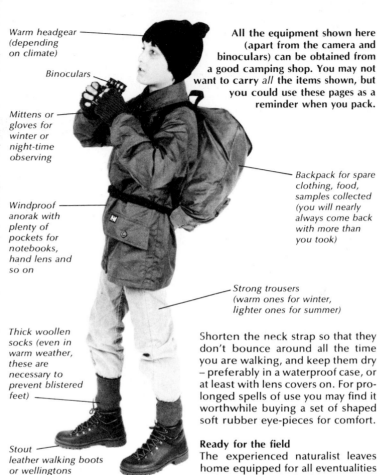

Warm headgear
(depending
on climate)

Binoculars

Mittens or
gloves for
winter or
night-time
observing

Windproof
anorak with
plenty of
pockets for
notebooks,
hand lens and
so on

Thick woollen
socks (even in
warm weather,
these are
necessary to
prevent blistered
feet)

Stout
leather walking boots
or wellingtons

All the equipment shown here
(apart from the camera and
binoculars) can be obtained from
a good camping shop. You may not
want to carry *all* the items shown, but
you could use these pages as a
reminder when you pack.

Backpack for spare
clothing, food,
samples collected
(you will nearly
always come back
with more than
you took)

Strong trousers
(warm ones for winter,
lighter ones for summer)

Shorten the neck strap so that they
don't bounce around all the time
you are walking, and keep them dry
– preferably in a waterproof case, or
at least with lens covers on. For pro-
longed spells of use you may find it
worthwhile buying a set of shaped
soft rubber eye-pieces for comfort.

Ready for the field
The experienced naturalist leaves
home equipped for all eventualities
and even though the beginner may
initially carry less specialized
equipment, he or she should be able
to stay warm and dry and able to
enjoy wildlife-watching to the full.
The safety rules are the same for
everyone and apply whether you are
in woodland, farmland, on the coast
or in bleak hill country. Dress sens-
ibly, tell someone where you are
going and when you will be back,
and take heed of weather forecasts
and the advice of local people.

For ease of carrying, lightweight
binoculars are preferable but when
making a selection pay great attention to lens quality. Look at the
straight edge of a building to check
that there is no bending or distortion
at the edge of the field of view. Also
look for any coloured fringes around
the image as these are signs of poor
quality lenses and are best avoided.

To keep your binoculars in good
condition don't knock or drop them.

Keeping a record

A well-kept notebook is one of the naturalist's most valuable assets. The permanent record of observations made during each day in the field builds up into a fund of information over the years. Notes and sketches of unfamiliar or unusual species make it possible for these to be looked up later in reference books, so you need never be left wondering what that strange fungus or insect really was.

The book should be a convenient pocket size, about 10×15cm, and ruled with feint lines. Either hardbacked or spiral-bound books can be used though hardbacks do last longer. An elastic band will keep the pages flat even in gusty winds. Use a pencil for notes and always carry a couple of spares. (Choose brightly painted ones or wrap coloured adhesive tape round them to make them show up when dropped.)

Using a system

A notebook entry is only valuable if it is complete – that is, if it will enable you or someone else to return to exactly the same spot to repeat the observation, and if the details in it are sufficient to allow accurate identification of the species you have observed.

Always start with the date, the exact location, and the time of day and make a note of the weather conditions and the type of habitat you are in (see opposite). Then make notes and sketches of the animals and plants around you, remembering to include as much detail as possible about colour, size and shape and, in the case of an animal, what it was doing and how it behaved if it caught sight of you. If it is a bird, note any plumage patterns on your sketches: a simple bird shape will do – you don't have to be an artist. Try to estimate the size of the bird by comparing a "new" bird with a familiar one like a sparrow or a pigeon. A good way to measure an insect is to watch which leaf it was sitting on and then measure the leaf after the insect has flown off.

Comparing notes

Sharing your notes and sketches with members of your local wildlife society is a good way to learn more. And sometimes the significance of your experiences may surprise you. Some years ago, in Devon, I saw a woodcock "roding" – that is, flying in a special way that is always associated with nesting. It was only when I mentioned this sighting to another enthusiast that I learnt that woodcock had not been seen nesting in the county for many years. I had almost overlooked an important and interesting observation!

▶ The page opposite was copied from the author's own field notebook and shows how sketches and brief notes are used to record the animals observed. Some naturalists use a spiral-bound notebook in the field and then make a neat copy in a hardbacked book later. A useful tip: mark a centimetre scale on the back cover for making quick measurements of leaves, insects and so on.

You can also transfer the notes and sketches from your field notebook into a number of separate books – one for butterflies, one for wild flowers, another for birds and so on; or you could compile an illustrated diary for each year. In future years, your "collected works" will provide you with both entertainment and facts.

Location : Haldon Devon — Rough grazing and conifer woodland.
Date : JULY 16 1979 (am)
warm day, light w-sw wind, few clouds.

Butterfly seen sunning itself on a bracken frond

v.dark green/brown upper surface

Ringlet × 1

Paler yellow/brown underside

wing underside

Butterflies also present

Grayling
Small heath
Meadow brown

conspicuous yellow ringed eyespots

Goldcrest × ½
Male or female ?

Very small birds,
Pale cream washed breast,
Yellow-green back
bead-like black eye

Bright yellow crest, black on either side

Short rounded wings and slightly forked tail

Double black and white wing bars

Amongst conifers

Photographing wildlife

The quality of any photograph depends as much on the photographer's skill as on his or her equipment and it would be a mistake to think that good results can only be achieved with very expensive cameras and lenses. A simple camera is often much better for a beginner because it allows more time to concentrate on the subject and on composition.

The ideal system
Assuming that a photographer has some experience and wishes to improve his or her results, the best choice will be a 35mm single lens reflex (SLR) camera, preferably with through-the-lens (TTL) light metering. This type of camera will take a wide range of lenses from wide-angle to telephoto. Lenses are very important: the camera may take the picture but the lens produces the results; one or two really good lenses are much better value than a lot of poor quality ones.

For the nature photographer an

▲ A close-up lens, or a close-up adaptor for a standard lens, is ideal for insect and flower shots.

ideal system would include a standard lens (35mm), a "macro" lens (50 or 90mm) for close work, a medium telephoto (135mm) and perhaps a long telephoto (300 or 400mm).

With practice, telephoto lenses can be hand-held even at quite slow shutter speeds but there are limits and if you use too slow a speed you will almost certainly have problems with camera movement. As a guide, never use speeds slower than 1/125 sec. with a 135mm lens and nothing slower than 1/500 sec. with a long lens like a 400mm. If you need to use slower speeds, use a tripod.

Keeping it simple
Excellent photographs can also be taken with a simple non-reflex camera. These have just one lens, although on some models an inexpensive close-up lens can be screwed onto the front of the fixed

lens. By pre-setting the closest focussing distance on the lens, a projecting wire may be used to check the distance between camera and subject for close-up shots. Most of these cameras also have a "bright-line" frame inside the viewfinder so that you can see exactly what will appear in the photograph.

Practice makes perfect

Many beginners suffer from camera shake and this can often be cured by using a faster shutter speed or by resting the camera on something solid like a wall or tree.

Experience is the key to success and although the "pot luck" approach – going for a walk with camera at the ready – will bring its share of good results, it is worth remembering that professional wildlife and natural history photographers plan their shots in advance, working out their hide position, the position of the sun, distances and likely exposures, before they even think of taking the first shot.

▲ In protected moorland habitats, wild ponies have little fear of man and will often approach within easy range of a standard lens. (So, too, will safari park animals.)

▼ A long focal-length lens, such as a 135mm, 150mm or 200mm telephoto, will enable you to fill the picture area (the "frame") even when you are photographing quite small animals.

Sounds natural

Headphones for monitoring sound

Lesser spotted woodpecker

Parabolic reflector

Cassette recorder

▲ Using a parabolic reflector, clear recordings of birdsong can be made at ranges of up to 30 metres.

Exploring the world of natural sound can add a new dimension to watching wildlife. Animals can produce a surprising range of sounds, and by no means all of them are vocal. There is the rasping of a snail's tongue, the noisy feeding of a hungry hedgehog, the warning "thump" of a rabbit and the summer sounds of grasshoppers and crickets. The breeding season brings the clash of deer antlers and the wing-clapping displays of some birds. Add to these the countless calls and songs of birds, mammals and frogs and the possibilities are endless.

What you need
For quality recordings the ideal machine is a portable reel-to-reel tape recorder. These, however, are very expensive. But almost as good are some of the newer lightweight

portable cassette recorders and here there is a wide range of choice.

When you are buying a recorder remember that you may have to carry it for long periods. Check it for weight (making sure that it has batteries in it at the time) and also find out how long one set of batteries will last. They can be an expensive item. The case should be strong, to give protection outdoors, and should give easy access to all the controls, even when being carried. The shoulder strap should be strongly sewn and fitted with a shoulder pad for comfort.

If possible use headphones to monitor the sound received by the microphone. Manual control of the recording level is preferable to automatic although today most portables are fully automatic.

Many recorders offer extras like

▲ **Keeping well hidden, a naturalist uses an imitation duck call to attract a flight of teal and mallard.**

Camouflage net

built-in microphones but these are not required for wildlife recording. Directional microphones can be very expensive but a parabolic reflector used with a standard "mike" will enable you to record at considerable distance from the subject. Here again, headphones are very useful as they let you check for background noises also collected by the reflector dish.

Play-back
Over the year you will be able to build up a library of bird calls and the more you play these back to yourself, the quicker and more reliable your field recognition will become. Always speak into the recorder at the end of a recording, giving the species, date, location and activity of the bird. If you record a bird but are unable to identify it, leave a gap on the tape. Later, you could "voice over" the details of the bird after checking its identity with another birdwatcher or by comparing it with pre-recorded tapes or records (see page 189).

Lore of the hunter
Many hunter's tricks can of course be used just as well by naturalists, and among them are various artificial calls that work by imitating the distress call of a prey species, the cry of a lost youngster, or by playing on the curiosity of many animals.

The clicking together of an old pair of antlers may attract a male deer to what he thinks is a rival in his territory. The imitated cry of an injured rabbit may bring fox or owl to the scene, and the fox may also come to a sucking sound made by the lips on the back of the hand.

149

Making a hide

Portable hide

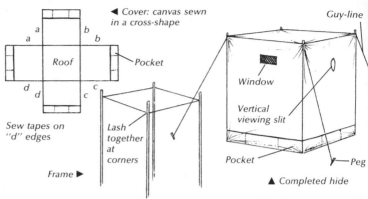

◄ Cover: canvas sewn in a cross-shape

Guy-line

a *b*

a *b*

Roof

Pocket

d *c*

d *c*

Sew tapes on "d" edges

Lash together at corners

Frame ►

Window

Vertical viewing slit

Pocket

Peg

▲ Completed hide

To make the *cover*, take two 430×100cm lengths of plain or camouflage-dyed light canvas and sew them together as shown. Turn up 15cm on each of the four edges to form *pockets* on the inside. Then stitch together sides aa, bb and cc, leaving a small gap at each corner of the roof for the poles to stick through. Sew the fourth side (dd) part-way down and attach *tapes* at 10cm intervals (thus making the entrance). Make the *frame* from eight poles, ideally hazel or ash, lashed tightly with strong string. Place the cover over the frame; stretch *guy-lines* tightly from the top of the poles to *pegs* angled in the earth. (On hard ground tie them to rocks). Stones in the pockets will prevent any flapping.

Cut short, vertical *viewing slits* in the side walls. (Horizontal slits sag open and reveal your movements). Hold the slit open with a sharpened twig "pricked" into the fabric (see opposite). "*Windows*" of fine dark mesh may be added but cover them with flaps inside when not in use.

A hide is simply an artificial hiding place built in order to allow observation of wildlife at close quarters. It can be made of natural materials such as bales of hay or straw, branches, reeds, or rocks and pieces of turf, but these should be used only with the permission of the landowner. Old farm equipment or abandoned vehicles will also provide good cover. It is worth remembering that the motor car makes an excellent mobile hide if driven up slowly and quietly (and if the occupants remain still inside and don't keep getting in and out).

Most useful of all, however, is the portable hide favoured by bird-watchers. It is simple to make and erect, and very versatile. A hide can be used at any time of the year but is most valuable during the breeding season when animals, and birds in particular, are at their most vulner-

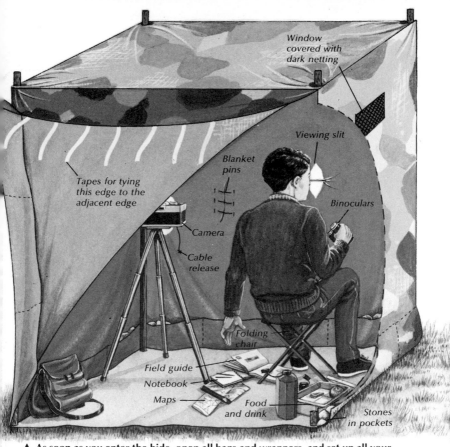

Window covered with dark netting

Viewing slit

Blanket pins

Tapes for tying this edge to the adjacent edge

Binoculars

Camera

Cable release

Folding chair

Field guide

Notebook

Maps

Food and drink

Stones in pockets

▲ As soon as you enter the hide, open all bags and wrappers, and set up all your equipment, to avoid noise later. Use blanket pins to close up gaps or slits that will not be needed, otherwise your movements may be seen.

able and nervous. The golden rule is that the hide should be introduced with the minimum of noise and disturbance. If a bird becomes unduly nervous, leave immediately. There is always another day.

It often causes less concern if you trick the bird into thinking you have gone away. Get someone to walk up to the hide with you and then ask them to walk away casually once you have slipped inside. A signal, such as a handkerchief hung outside the hide door, will tell your friend when to "collect" you again.

Outside the breeding season there is little danger of causing distress and a good place to start observing is at a pond or estuary where wildfowl or waders come to feed. There you can practise using the hide and also develop other skills like identifying birds in a mixed flock and estimating numbers.

ATTRACTING WILDLIFE

Baits, lights and lures

Once you have a good idea of what animals are living in your area – by locating their tracks, droppings, feeding signs, or other "clues" – it may well be possible to attract some of them into more open areas where you can get a better look at them. Many species live in well-hidden, inaccessible burrows (and with good reason) but a little cunning, skill, and fieldcraft may tempt them into full view.

The most obvious trick is to lay bait but for this to be successful the baiting must be carried out regularly, in the right place, and with the right bait for the particular animal sought.

Outfoxing the fox

Foxes will eat almost anything once they have been attracted to a regular baiting site. At the side of a well-used route, or "run", is usually a good place. Start by putting out a rabbit carcass (a road casualty will do perfectly), then introduce kitchen scraps like bread and fish. Foxes have, in fact, become so well adapted to living close to man that they are quite often seen in towns where they tend to put aside hunting in favour of scavenging in dustbins. But although the urban fox has become bold, his country relatives are still amongst the wariest of animals, and bait is best laid where it can be seen from a hide, preferably built well above ground in a tree or in an outbuilding.

Choosing the bait

Badgers, like foxes, will eat just about anything you offer but they

▲ *Good vibrations:* **the secretive wall spider lives in a silk-lined hole but can often be tricked into the open by touching one of its radiating "trip wires" with a tuning fork! Like all spiders it is highly sensitive to vibration and so – mistaking the vibrations for the frantic struggles of a trapped fly – it dashes to the attack. Its retreat may be temporarily blocked by placing a twig across the hole.**

are particulary attracted to a rich mixture made of peanuts and honey. Wood mice can be lured by a bait of seeds and cereals. Bank voles will come to chopped carrot and cereals, while field voles seem to prefer pieces of turnip and apple, a combination also relished by the water vole. In areas where squirrels are used to making raids on garden bird-tables their greed can easily be turned to advantage by putting out a mixture of nuts – oak, beech, hazel, chestnut and peanuts.

Scavenging birds can be attracted to a convenient part of an open field by a rabbit carcass, tethered to a stake to prevent it being carried away. Ideally, the bait should be

Silver Y

Brimstone

Common wainscot

Large yellow underwing

Broad-bordered yellow underwing

▲ *Night lures:* by the time the last post has been painted with the sugar solution, the first has already attracted a selection of moths and more are arriving every minute. Try sugaring on warm nights between June and August. There are usually two spells of activity, the first about two hours after sunset and the second starting around one in the morning.

placed near the edge of the field so that you can watch from the cover of a hedge or from a temporary hide made of straw bales, hurdles, or any other material familiar to these very suspicious birds.

Sweetness and light

Birds and mammals are not alone in falling for bait, and one very good way to observe moths is by "sugaring" a line of posts or trees. The main ingredients of the bait are something to give the mixture "body", a small amount of alcohol (to make the moths feel "drowsy"), and a powerful attractant. Many entomologists have their own favourite recipes but a simple one

would be: 4 tablespoons of black treacle, 2 tablespoons of beer, and 1 teaspoon of amyl acetate ("pear-drops"). The mixture should be kept in a tightly stoppered jar until required. On a warm, still, "muggy" summer's night, paint the mixture onto the posts in stripes about 2cm wide by 30cm long (see above).

An alternative method is to play on the attractiveness of light. Most purpose-built moth-traps are expensive, but for beginners a simple lure can be made from a white sheet laid on the ground beneath a powerful incandescent light like a "Tilley" lamp. Once the insects have been identified, they are released, preferably close to cover.

The garden sanctuary

Most hobbies and interests begin at home and wildlife watching need not be any different. Even in the midst of the city there is a host of birdlife to be seen; many species can be attracted by putting up nest-boxes, and by putting out suitable food in the hard winter months.

Our very tidy gardening habits are often not much help to insects, many of which need the nettles, michaelmas daisies, thistles, and dandelions that are all too often branded as weeds. For many insects such plants provide them with nectar, egg-laying sites, and food for their larvae. If your garden is big enough, try letting the bottom end, or a hidden corner, go back to the semi-wild state by planting woodland and hedgerow plants that are native to this country, and some of the shrubs and perennials that are typical of the country cottage garden. The illustration shows some of the many other ways you can make a garden more attractive to wildlife.

Mammal life is less well adapted to urban life; however, in areas near parks, recreation grounds and public commons, and particularly in suburban areas where the open countryside is not too far away, it is quite possible for a garden to attract a number of mammal visitors – especially if the garden itself is safe and well supplied with plant and insect food and warm, dry places to make a home. You are not very likely to have a fox or badger take up residence but you may find that a pile of plant-pots and garden odds and ends has provided a safe, sheltered home for a hedgehog family or that frogs, toads or newts are breeding in your garden pond. And if they are, don't restock the pond with fish, which will compete for food. Our native amphibians need all the help they can get as natural ponds are drained, polluted, or filled up with domestic rubbish.

Ivy (good nesting site)

Holly blue

Wren

Holly

Honeysuckle (attracts insects)

Common toad

Eyed hawk moth

Comma

Painted lady

Long grass and "weeds"

Robin

Hedgehog

Leaf litter

Nettles

Woodpigeon

Trees and shrubs provide cover
and nesting sites for birds

House
sparrow

House
martin

Chaffinch

Blue tit
and nest
box

Bird table:
put out food
in winter

Blackbird

Flowers to
attract insects

Thrush

Red admiral

Sallow

Buddleia
(attracts
butterflies)

Pond with
water plants

Grey
squirrel

Peacock
butterfly

Common
frog

Small
tortoiseshell

Convolvulus
hawk moth on
tobacco plant
(a garden flower)

Bee log
(see page 139)

Duke of Burgundy
fritillary on
primrose

Cinnabar moth
caterpillars
on ragwort

155

The woodland mammals

Badgers

If there are badgers in your local woods they should not be too hard to find. Look first for the large sett, dug into a bank or the side of a slope. A large pile of excavated earth will spill down the slope from the main entrance and in many cases a furrow scraped in the earth will show where the busy animal has moved surplus soil well away from the entrance. The complex burrow may extend more than three metres below ground, with a number of separate chambers linked by tunnels. The badger is a wary and cunning animal and every sett will have a number of alternative entrances.

Then check for signs that the sett is in use. Fresh tracks and marks of digging are clear signs, especially in spring and summer. You may also find scratch marks on trees near the sett. To check which entrance is being used, lay a few small sticks across likely holes and call back the next day to see which have been moved. Alternatively, wind some adhesive tape, sticky side out, around an exposed root or firmly-planted stick, just inside the sett entrance. A passing badger will leave hairs on the tape.

Badgers are unusually clean and tidy animals so look around for the shallow latrine holes they make. Fresh droppings will confirm that the sett is occupied. Small piles of dry grass and bracken show that the

▶ The features illustrated in this picture will enable you to identify a badger sett that is in use.

old bedding has been cleared out and replaced by fresh dry grass. Well worn areas of ground may indicate where the young badgers play, and flattened vegetation will reveal paths that are in regular use.

Getting into position

Always choose your observation point in advance – and in daylight. Ideally you want a comfortable fork in a stout tree, about ten metres from the sett and two metres above ground so that any swirling wind is likely to carry your scent over the badger's head.

Badgers can be observed at almost any time of year. They do not hibernate though they are less active in winter. However, for those keen on seeing cubs, late April, May and June are the best months. Dress warmly and be in position by 9.00 pm. The animals will usually emerge soon after dark: if not, it is well worth waiting as they are sometimes slow to get moving. Often you will hear the most surprising noises for badgers are very vocal, grunting and

Main entrance

Adult badger

Excavated earth

Cubs at play

Old bedding

_____ Path used by badgers

snorting and even making a sound like the clucking of a coot. After checking the air for danger, the family will usually stay near the sett for a short while before moving off to forage for food.

Hedgehogs

The hedgehog is one of the most appealing of our wild animals and also one of the easiest to watch. Although basically a nocturnal animal it differs from the badger in starting its activities usually around dusk instead of waiting for darkness. However, hedgehogs may also be seen in broad daylight – especially when a long dry spell is broken by a refreshing downpour and there are plenty of slugs and snails about.

Look for the animal's footprints in the earth bank at the side of a country road, or along the base of a hedge. Look also around farm buildings and haystacks as well as among the thick roots of woodland trees where the hedgehog likes to make its nest. Most of the day is spent fast asleep but once it is awake the hedgehog can cover quite a distance in its nightly wandering. If you get

into position early, armed with your red-filtered torch, you will be able to follow its journey easily. Hedgehogs are tolerant creatures and so long as you walk softly it will not take fright.

In this way you can watch it feed, carefully noting what prey is taken and how the hedgehog deals with it. In addition to slugs and snails the very broad diet includes frogs, birds' eggs and nestlings, earthworms, mice and also a variety of berries, nuts and fruits.

The hedgehog is also an important predator on baby rabbits and this tough little hunter will tackle animals as large and fierce as rats with remarkable success. However, against foxes and badgers the hedgehog uses its own very special technique – rolling into a tight ball and presenting its attacker with a painful wall of sharp spines. The defensive prickles also serve another useful purpose. Hedgehogs are good climbers but are better going up than down: to descend, they roll into a ball and drop to the ground – the spines acting as an efficient shock-absorber so they bounce gently then unroll and scurry off unharmed.

Between three and seven blind, helpless young are born in a warm nest of moss and leaves, usually between May and July. A second litter may be born in early autumn but for them it is a race against time: they must put on plenty of weight if they are to be able to hibernate safely through the winter.

▼ If you don't crowd a hedgehog too much, you may be able to follow it for miles as it hunts for food.

Scratch marks

Rear exit of badger sett

Hedgehog's nest of moss and leaves

Badger's latrine

Hedgehog

157

Red squirrel, grey squirrel

In Britain we have the native red squirrel, which is also found all over Europe, and the slightly bigger grey squirrel, introduced from America during the last century. Disease had reduced the number of red squirrels even before the grey ones arrived, and when the number of red squirrels eventually grew again, the grey squirrel became the more common in most areas.

The best time of year to watch these delightful little animals is in the late summer and early part of autumn as they search for food among the leaf litter and collect nuts and beech mast from the trees. As winter approaches and the trees lose their dense covering of leaves the squirrels are much easier to watch as they scamper along the branches with amazing agility, sometimes leaping over three metres from one tree to the next. Their sharp claws provide a sure grip and the bushy tail acts as a balancing aid.

The red squirrel prefers conifer forest although it also inhabits deciduous woodlands – especially beechwoods. The grey prefers beech, oak and hazel woods although it too may be found in conifers. Both make a spherical nest known as a "drey" (see above). It is made of woven twigs, lined with

Red squirrel and drey

moss, leaves and strips of bark. The squirrel usually makes one large main winter nest, in which the young are born, and also a number of smaller ones which serve as temporary sleeping quarters.

The main foods are acorns, pine seeds, beech mast and hazelnuts, but squirrels will also take wild cherries, the bark and young shoots of pine trees, and birds' eggs and nestlings. The marks left by the squirrel on nut shells and cones are very distinctive (see below) and most wildlife watchers will very quickly learn to recognize them. The most certain clue to the presence of squirrels is the carpet of feeding litter spread on the ground beneath a favourite tree.

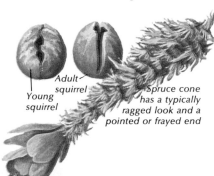

Adult squirrel

Young squirrel

Spruce cone has a typically ragged look and a pointed or frayed end

◀ Signs of feeding by squirrels on hazelnuts and a spruce cone. The squirrel gnaws a notch across the end of a hazelnut then puts its lower incisors into the crack and levers the shell open. Young animals take time to learn the trick and their teeth-marks are not nearly as neat as the adults'.

Wood mouse, shrew

The wood mouse is also called the long-tailed field mouse, and with good reason for it is equally at home in woodland, field, hedgerow or garden – anywhere, in fact, that provides plenty of ground cover.

Its large black eyes give an immediate clue to the fact that it is mainly a nocturnal animal, and watching one at night by the light of a red-filtered torch is certainly the most rewarding way to see one. However, the wood mouse can also be enticed out in daylight by laying bait beside one of its regular "runs". These pathways are often more like tunnels for the animal likes to keep under cover. It will, however, climb into a bush to get at a crop of ripe berries and will make surprising leaps, or bound away like a miniature kangaroo, if danger threatens.

The wood mouse feeds on all kinds of berries, nuts, acorns and seeds and will also take worms, grubs, insects and spiders. Food is often hoarded away in large quantities in the mouse's underground burrows. The breeding nest is safely underground, but during the summer shallow burrows may be used, and nests may even be made above ground. Occasionally wood mice will raid gardens to feed on flower bulbs and crops of peas.

Wood mouse

Shrew

The **common shrew** is usually heard before it is seen – giving itself away by its shrill squeaking or chattering. It is one of our smallest mammals – forever on the move, and forever eating. It is active by day and by night, alternately sleeping and feeding around the clock.

The shrew's long twitching nose is perfect for snuffling among the leaf litter for insects and worms but it will quite often climb up grass stems and into bushes to catch insects. The winter is spent under the leaf litter but in summer the shrew is likely to be found out in fields and meadows and near hedgerows, and the ball-shaped nest of grass is often placed in the bank of a ditch or in the tangle of growth at the foot of a hedge.

▶ **The tell-tale signs of a wood mouse that has been feeding. It is much neater than a squirrel, nibbling cones smooth and leaving no ragged fibres or rough scales. And instead of scattering the debris around, as a squirrel would, the mouse carries the cone away to a quiet feeding place.**

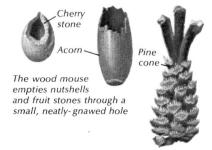

Cherry stone

Acorn

Pine cone

The wood mouse empties nutshells and fruit stones through a small, neatly-gnawed hole

A third-year roebuck moves quietly through the woodland browsing on leaves, shoots and shrubs, and grazing on grasses, fungi and a variety of forest floor plants. It is early spring and the buck is in velvet. Roe are active day and night but feed mainly in the early morning – often retiring into dense cover around midday.

Right forefoot

4cm

Deer

In addition to the native red deer and roe deer, several other species have been introduced into Britain. They include fallow deer, sika deer, muntjak and Chinese water deer. Deer parks offer the easiest way of observing these beautiful woodland animals but even where they are used to man's presence they are often still very shy.

Stalking requires skill and patience. The approach must be silent, always from the downwind side, and in dense cover as far as possible. (See page 168 for watching red deer in highland country and page 138 for alarm signals.) In many areas occupied by deer there are permanent viewing positions ("high-seats") placed in trees, so remember to ask about these when requesting permission to go on private land. One more important rule is that you should leave as carefully as you arrived. If deer are alarmed they will stay away from that area for days.

Each year the male deer replaces his antlers – his fighting weapons and the symbols of his strength and importance. The new antlers are at first covered with skin, known as "velvet" but as soon as they have hardened the velvet is "frayed" – that is, rubbed off by thrashing the antlers against a bush or sapling. The damage caused by fraying is one of the most dramatic animal signs. Roe deer also leave another characteristic sign when the buck marks his territory with scent from a gland on his forehead (see page 137).

In most species the old antlers are cast in the spring and the new ones frayed in late summer or early autumn. Roe deer are the odd ones out in casting in November and fraying in the spring. Cast-off antlers make fine trophies but unfortunately they are cast one at a time. Only where an animal has died might you find the two antlers together.

Other signs to watch for are the characteristic cloven hoof prints, the animals' droppings, and their regular pathways through the woodland and clearings. Roe deer are very fond of chasing around in circles, especially in the rut, so if you find a circular path – often round a tree or isolated rock – you have found a promising observation point.

Pipistrelle bat

Entice a bat into close range by flicking a tiny pebble into its path as it swoops after insects. Detecting the pebble by echo-location, the bat will often dive to investigate – sometimes taking a couple of turns round the falling object before deciding that it is not a tasty meal after all. A bat may even swoop at an angler's cast.

Bats

Bats are fascinating creatures to watch, for despite the "horror film" image they have been given, they are very clean animals, quite harmless, and also unique among mammals in being the only mammal group to have mastered the art of flying.

The bat's wing is supported by the very long finger bones, not the arm bones as might be expected, and its flight is far more agile than that of even the most acrobatic bird. At full speed it can virtually stop, spin round, somersault and flash away in another direction as it hunts in the gathering dusk for night-flying moths and other insects. Prey are seized in the mouth or scooped up with the wing or the membrane between the back legs, and then transferred to the mouth. The bat's remarkable echo-location system enables it to home in on its prey with deadly accuracy and to fly swiftly among trees in complete darkness without hitting anything.

During the day bats retire to their roosts in caves, hollow trees, and buildings. Church belfries and old warehouses are "traditional" roosts but quite recently bats were found to have taken up residence in the cavity walls of the houses on a new estate. The best place to watch for bats is near a suitable roosting place, often given away by the animals' droppings. The bats usually stream out to hunt as darkness falls. All British species are now protected.

▲ Greater horseshoe bats hang upside down in clusters from the roof of a cave. Hibernation is from October until March or April, but in a very cold spring it may continue into May or even into June.

161

Watching at night

This observer has prepared a safe and comfortable place in a tree in order to watch woodland animals at night. While you don't need a high seat to see a mouse, you need to be well clear of the ground in order to avoid detection by other animals such as badgers. The scent of this observer will be carried above the heads of any ground-dwelling animals.

Try night-watching in other well-populated habitats such as dense hedgerows, using the techniques of locating, attracting and observing wildlife explained elsewhere in this book.

Permanent padded seat

Wood mouse attracted by bait
Hedgehog

Watching wildlife at night is a rewarding pastime, not at all sinister as some people's imagination would have them believe. Sitting quite still, it is remarkable how much can be heard and, once your eyes have become accustomed to the darkness, how much can be seen as well.

Torches should be used very sparingly at night as they will ruin your night vision for several minutes after they have been switched off. You can, however, modify an ordinary torch for night use by fixing a red filter (or a piece of red cellophane) over the lens. Most animals seem completely unaware of red light.

Creatures of the night
Many of our native animals are nocturnal by habit, emerging under cover of darkness to hunt or forage for food. The badger, for instance, is truly nocturnal, rarely emerging until well after sunset whereas the hedgehog is already busy at dusk (see pages 156–7). The common dormouse actively forages at night for food, often climbing trees on woodland edges to do so, but this charming little creature is extremely difficult to see. However, some small rodents, such as wood mice, can be attracted by bait.

Much easier to spot are the many invertebrates that are active at night: moths being the most varied in shape and colour (see page 153). Other invertebrates, such as slugs, woodlice and centipedes, need to avoid losing moisture during the day, and are therefore less active

Bats leaving roost in old mill

Nightjar hawking after moths

Barn owl hunting rodents

Badger emerging from wood

Fox with rabbit

than during the normally cooler, damper nights. They can be seen in the leaf litter, or even climbing the bark of the trees in search of food.

In contrast there are very few birds abroad at night. The haunting hoot of a tawny owl and the piercing screech of a barn owl are sounds to remember, but even more thrilling is the sight of an owl twisting and turning among the trees or along the hedgerows in its hunting flight. In heathland and woodland clearings in summer a really fortunate observer may even see a nightjar.

Dusk is also the time to watch and listen for bats, for although the noises they make in order to locate their prey are too high-pitched for us to hear, their alarm signals *can* be picked up by the human ear.

Safety First

Being out at night obviously requires care, good sense, and preparation – so follow the code of safe conduct.

1 Never go out alone.
2 Make sure that someone at home knows *exactly* where you are going, and when you intend returning.
3 Get to know the study area very well in daylight. It is all too easy to become disorientated in darkness.
4 Wrap up well, including a hat and gloves, and take a hot drink and food with you.
5 Carry a whistle in addition to a torch in case of emergency.

Exploring an oak tree

Look at an old oak tree. From a distance it is a magnificent sight with its massive trunk dividing again and again into the gnarled and twisted branches of its huge spreading canopy.

Look again, and you begin to see signs of life. Birds fly in and out carrying nesting materials, or food for their young. A squirrel runs along a branch and disappears from sight, startling a great spotted woodpecker that had been exploring a patch of rotten wood.

Closer still and you can see ants, beetles, spiders and centipedes running about over the rough surface of the bark while greenfly, caterpillars and an assortment of strange-looking bugs fly, jump and wriggle among the leaves. Some of these insects chew the leaves, some pierce them to suck the juices inside, while others are there mainly to lay their eggs. Some are hunters, some the hunted – this single tree is like a forest in its own right.

Borers and miners
Out of sight beneath the bark the borers are at work. Several kinds of beetle and their larvae, and even the caterpillars of certain moths, live inside the trunk and branches of the living tree. Some make shallow tunnels just below the bark while others tunnel deep into the heart of the tree causing a great deal of damage. Leaves too are attacked by "miners". The larvae of weevils, sawflies and tiny moths known as "micros" tunnel inside the leaf, feeding on the soft green flesh without breaking through the tough outer skin.

Other insects cause galls to form on leaves, buds, twigs and even on roots below ground. The gall is a mass of plant tissue, usually in the shape of a ball or plate, that forms as a reaction to insect eggs or grubs. They do no lasting harm to the tree but provide shelter and a neat food-store for the insects.

Plants without soil
There are plants, too, that grow high up on the tree rather than on the ground. They are called "epiphytes" and range from the green powdery lichen that commonly covers the trunk, to a dozen different mosses and a wide variety of ferns, herbs and other flowering plants. These are all green plants, able to manufacture their food from sunlight and from the nutrients absorbed through their roots. Also common on oak trees are various kinds of fungi. Unlike the green plants, these have no chlorophyll of their own and so they live as "parasites" – taking their food from the tree (and sometimes causing its death) or else living off rotten wood or the decaying leaves carpeting the ground below.

Things to do
A single tree offers a huge range of fascinating projects (see opposite for some suggestions).

You can also make a collection of epiphytes and then try to work out how they came to be in the tree. Were they carried by the wind, or by birds perhaps? Another area to inspect is the soil around the roots of an oak. Here you may find large grubs of insects, which could be kept for observation in a subterrarium (see page 167).

Tree studies make ideal group projects so why not involve your friends, or become a member of one of the many naturalists' clubs?

▼ *Collecting and hatching galls*
Dozens of gall-producing insects live on oak trees and although the insects themselves are tiny and hard to find, the galls they cause are often brightly coloured or at least large enough to be seen easily. They can be kept in a dry, well-ventilated jar until the adult flies emerge.

▼ *Bark and gallery rubbings*
If you see a piece of loose bark, lift it carefully to see if anything has made a home beneath it. (And replace it just as carefully when you have finished.) If you find the galleries of an oak bark beetle, try making a rubbing with paper and a crayon or soft pencil. You can also make bark rubbings.

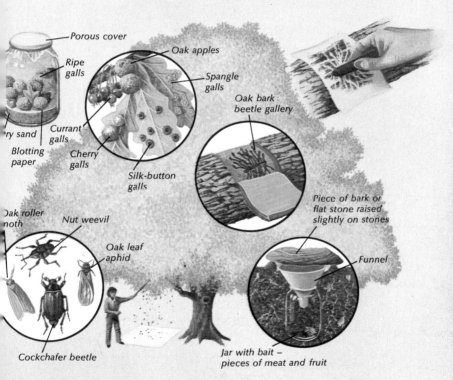

Porous cover

Ripe galls

Oak apples

Spangle galls

Oak bark beetle gallery

ry sand

Currant galls

Blotting paper

Cherry galls

Silk-button galls

Piece of bark or flat stone raised slightly on stones

Oak roller moth

Nut weevil

Oak leaf aphid

Funnel

Cockchafer beetle

Jar with bait – pieces of meat and fruit

▲ *Tree-life survey*
Place a white sheet beneath a low branch and then beat or shake the branch to dislodge the creatures living in it. Sort the galls, grubs, caterpillars and so on into groups and count them, identifying as many as you can. Make sketches of the animal life for your records.

▲ *Leaf litter surveys*
Cut the spout from a wide funnel, place it in the neck of a large jar containing bait, and bury them in the soil under a tree as shown. Insects will slip into the jar and be trapped. Check your trap often to avoid starving the insects, and remove the trap (or seal the top) in rainy weather

165

The forest floor

If you look closely at the many different plants that make up a wood, you will find that what looks at first like an untidy jumble of vegetation is, in fact, quite neatly organized. Usually it is possible to pick out four distinct layers, one above the other.

The upper layer (or *canopy*) is formed by the trees themselves. They support a wealth of animal life, and plant life too, but just as importantly they affect everything beneath them by shading the ground, protecting it from wind and excessive frost, and by shedding a carpet of leaves. Below the canopy comes the *shrub layer*, sometimes very dense, sometimes quite thin. In some broadleaved woods, for example, the tangle of brambles and hornbeam, hawthorn and hazel provides cover for a variety of birds and an ideal place for spiders to spin their webs.

Closer to the ground lies a rich *herb layer* made up of grasses and nettles and familiar woodland flowers. And last of all comes the *ground layer*, consisting of mosses and other ground-hugging plants, and also the *leaf litter*, slowly decomposing and adding to the soil.

Woodland low-life

Woodland leaf litter tends to be overlooked by many naturalists and yet in broadleaved woods it teems with animal life of all kinds. No sooner does a leaf fall to the ground than it begins the process of breakdown that will eventually return all its useful nutrients and fibre to the soil.

Woodlice, millipedes and a great variety of worms are among the plant feeders that help break down the leaf material, while that same thick layer of debris gives cover to hunting insects like the centipedes, hunting spiders and numerous beetles. Many of the ground beetles are glossy black with a dramatic green, bronze or purple sheen, and some have stink glands in their defensive armory. Scurrying about in the leaf litter, under flakes of bark, and among mossy ground vegetation, they hunt for worms, grubs and other insects. However, even more fearsome than the beetles are some of their own larvae. The tiger beetle larva, for example, is a strange creature that lives in the mouth of a vertical burrow in the soil. When some unfortunate insect strays too close, the larva pounces and drags its prey underground.

Many of the smaller creatures of the forest floor are well worth a close look and specimens can be collected quite easily with simple traps. Pieces of tree bark or hollowed-out grapefruit halves can be placed on the ground, but best of all is a jar sunk in the soil below a slippery plastic funnel placed with its edge level with the ground (see page 165).

A few minutes' digging with a small trowel, especially around the base of a large tree, will usually produce a variety of large larvae and earthworms, many of which can be kept in a subterrarium like the one shown opposite.

Habitats to study

Even a short walk along a woodland path is likely to provide a number of interesting micro-habitats – the name used for small areas in which, for various reasons, conditions are not the same as in the overall habitat.

Inside a wood you could make a

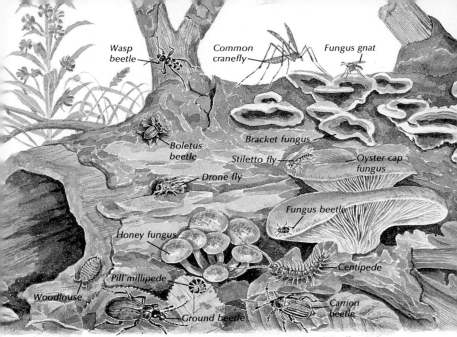

Wasp beetle — Common cranefly — Fungus gnat — Boletus beetle — Bracket fungus — Stiletto fly — Oyster cap fungus — Drone fly — Fungus beetle — Honey fungus — Centipede — Pill millipede — Woodlouse — Ground beetle — Carrion beetle

▲ In the ten years that went by between falling to the ground and finally rotting away to powder, this large branch section provided food, breeding sites and shelter to dozens of animal and plant species.

detailed study, preferably repeated at intervals, of a decaying log. All the insects and plants growing on and around the log should be noted but samples should not be removed and any pieces of log that are moved should be replaced with great care exactly as they were.

A similar study can be made of any small mammal or bird carcass and this will provide an opportunity to watch the activities of the various sexton beetles in addition to ground beetles and many flies. Nothing is wasted. The flesh disappears very quickly but even bone and feather will rot away in a few months.

Even a pile of animal droppings will soon accumulate a number of interesting insects, in addition to the birds who prey on the dung-beetles and flies.

Subterrarium

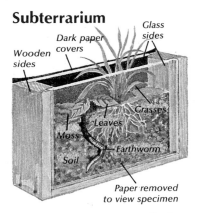

Glass sides — Dark paper covers — Wooden sides — Grasses — Leaves — Moss — Earthworm — Soil — Paper removed to view specimen

▲ The subterrarium is usually kept dark by the black paper covers but these can be removed to observe the specimen and to take photographs or make sketches.

167

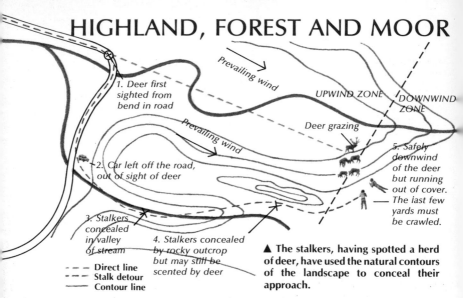

1. Deer first sighted from bend in road

Prevailing wind

UPWIND ZONE

DOWNWIND ZONE

Deer grazing

2. Car left off the road, out of sight of deer

Prevailing wind

5. Safely downwind of the deer but running out of cover. The last few yards must be crawled.

3. Stalkers concealed in valley of stream

4. Stalkers concealed by rocky outcrop but may still be scented by deer

- - - Direct line
- - - Stalk detour
——— Contour line

▲ The stalkers, having spotted a herd of deer, have used the natural contours of the landscape to conceal their approach.

Red Deer

Although red deer may be seen in several parts of lowland Britain, the best place to watch them is in the dramatic hill country of the Scottish Highlands and Islands.

In winter, when there is little grazing to be had on the snow-covered hills, the deer will often come right down into the valleys, even to the roadside. Then, a car makes an effective hide if it is driven up slowly and quietly and if the occupants remain quiet and still.

In summer the deer roam far out onto the high moors and a long and careful stalk is necessary (see above). The deer has excellent vision, good hearing, and a very sensitive nose. If you see deer at the head of a glen and the wind is behind you, start your detour immediately – even if the animals are a couple of miles away. To avoid alerting them you will have to swing round in a wide arc, always keeping out of sight, until

your scent can no longer be carried to them on the breeze. Walk softly, without chattering, and avoid any patches of loose stones on the hillside. Always crawl forward and take a careful look *before* you go over the top of a rise. And whenever you are in view of the deer, watch them closely – especially the stag and leading hind. If they stop feeding or look towards you, freeze flat on the ground until they relax. Once frightened they will be off over the hill and may not settle again until they are miles away.

If possible, go out with an experienced stalker during September or early October when the rut is at its peak. The sight and sound of a big stag challenging potential rivals is an unforgettable experience, especially in the half-light of dusk or early morning (see page 140). At this time of year, look out also for muddy pools and boggy areas churned up and surrounded by hoof prints. The stags love to wallow and there can be few more dramatic sights than a stag heaving himself out of a wallow, dripping water and mud like some huge prehistoric beast.

Highland country is beautiful but should be treated with respect. Twenty minutes can see a change from warm sunshine to bitter winds or swirling mists, so dress warmly and keep an eye on the weather. If possible, go with an experienced person. It is safer by far, and you will learn much more. You may even be lucky enough to be shown the field signs of one of the rarer highland animals.

Wild Cat

The northern Highlands are home to Britain's only wild member of the cat family. Larger and more powerfully built than the domestic cat, the wild cat lies up during the day in its lair among the hillside rocks but travels far and wide in its nightly hunts.

The cat preys on hares and rabbits, grouse and other birds, and may even take lambs and very young or weak deer calves. You will be lucky to see the cat itself but look out for prints – like those of a domestic cat but a little larger – and also for droppings. Like its domestic relative, the wild cat buries its droppings within its own territory, but around the edges of its territory it will leave them on top of rocks or grass tussocks to act as a warning to any other cat who wanders into the area.

Wild cats usually hunt alone, or occasionally in pairs – prowling the hillsides and mountain forests at dawn and dusk as they seek their prey. They are seldom seen but their harsh, unearthly cries are often heard as hunting cats call to each other.

▲ This red squirrel was no match for the swift and agile marten.

Pine Marten

Even more rare is this large member of the weasel family. In ages past it was common throughout the woodlands of Britain but hunting and trapping greatly reduced its numbers. It is now found only in the hill country of northern England, Wales and Scotland, but in some areas it is thought to be on the increase.

The pine marten spends most of its time in the trees, preying on squirrels and birds, but it will also come down to the ground to hunt rats and mice and rabbits. Like all members of the stoat/weasel group it is a fearless and fearsome predator – quite capable of tackling prey larger than itself.

The marten is protected and on no account should it be disturbed. If you are lucky enough to see one, *don't* tell everyone around – but *do* let one of the main conservation organizations know of the sighting (see addresses later in this book).

GRASSLAND AND FARMLAND

Although grasslands may appear much the same at first glance they vary a great deal in the variety of plant life they support and the amount of food and cover they offer to animals.

Richest of all are old meadows and pasture lands and you can recognize these by the large number of anthills underfoot, skylarks overhead and by a general richness of wild flowers and their associated insects – bees, flies, butterflies and grasshoppers. Mature limestone and chalk grasslands are drier and have their own characteristic plants and insects.

Along with natural grassland we must also consider farmland. Fields of turnips offer a feast to animals as different as badgers, voles and deer, while grass crops like wheat, oats and barley attract mice and voles and countless seed-eating birds – often to the great annoyace of the farmer. The boundaries between different types of farmland, often marked by hedges, ditches or small clusters of trees, also provide opportunities for wildlife communities to develop and flourish (see pages 176–7).

The grassland mammals

Wild rabbit

One of our most familiar animals is the rabbit, and yet only 30 years ago it was almost wiped out by the virus disease myxomatosis. In some areas 99 per cent of the wild rabbits died but they are now recovering.

Where the population is still low, the rabbits often live above ground and this makes them difficult to watch at close range, but where the numbers are larger the rabbits live in the more familiar warrens.

Rabbits are most active at dawn and dusk and the best way to watch them is from a nearby tree, or better still from a hide built on stilts right in the middle of the warren. You could also use a wall or hedge as cover but if possible get above their level – they have a very good sense of smell.

To stop them wandering off to feed, place small heaps of rabbit pellets near the burrows. You can buy them from any pet shop and the wild

▼ A large rabbit warren is an ideal place to study animal behaviour.

Scattered earth shows where a badger has raided a "stop" and killed the young rabbits

Main warren

Young rabbit in alert posture outside its nursery burrow

Small mounds or anthills may be used as latrine areas, especially by the dominant males in the colony

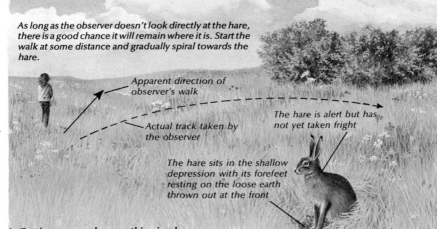

As long as the observer doesn't look directly at the hare, there is a good chance it will remain where it is. Start the walk at some distance and gradually spiral towards the hare.

Apparent direction of observer's walk

Actual track taken by the observer

The hare is alert but has not yet taken fright

The hare sits in the shallow depression with its forefeet resting on the loose earth thrown out at the front

▲ **Getting near a hare – this simple trick can be effective in open country.**

rabbits love them. A rabbit warren offers plenty of scope for studying behaviour, especially in March, April and May – the height of the breeding season. Try to work out the family groups within the colony, and the order of rank within each family. Look also for the nursery burrow, called a "stop", that the female digs some distance away from the main warren. If you have a well-placed observation position you will be able to watch the doe visiting the stop to feed her young, and later you will see the youngsters make their first excursions into the outside world.

Brown hare

Unlike the rabbit, the hare is a solitary animal for much of the time although males (jacks) and females (does) may be seen together throughout the spring breeding season.

Hares are creatures of habit, always crossing hedges and walls at the same places and sticking to favourite tracks. Careful watching and noting of footprints will tell you the best place to put your tree-seat

or build your hide.

If you see a hare in open ground you can try another tactic. Walk along steadily, in full view but at an angle to the hare and without looking directly at it. If you keep altering your line towards the animal you will walk in a spiral round it but you will always appear to be walking past, minding your own business. Like all field tricks it doesn't always work but sometimes it will bring you surprisingly close.

The lowland (brown) hare rests in a shallow depression called a form, usually well hidden among long grass, but the closely related Scottish mountain, or arctic, hare makes more use of natural cover and often hides in crevices among rocks. Like the stoat, the Scottish hare turns white in winter.

In either case watch for the remarkable behaviour of the doe as she approaches or leaves her young. To break her tell-tale scent trail she will make sudden enormous leaps at right-angles to her direction of travel, sometimes springing onto a bank or wall, or out into a patch of marshy ground to kill the scent.

An area of farmland containing a mixture of cornfields and pasture land, damp meadow and marshland, provides the perfect setting in which to look for our smaller mammal species. Moles inhabit the well-drained pastures, the field vole (or field mouse) likes damp grassland areas, while the agile little harvest mouse prefers tall vegetation like the long-stemmed marsh grasses, and crops such as wheat.

Mole

Although few of us ever see a mole we are all familiar with its field signs – the conspicuous mounds of earth that are dotted around arable land and pasture.

For its size the mole must be among the strongest of animals, able to burrow through the soil at a fast rate in its ceaseless hunt for earthworms, leather-jackets, wire-worms and other insect larvae. It burns up energy so fast that it must eat right round the clock, alternating bouts of frantic activity with short rest periods spent in its nest chamber. This is usually just below ground level beneath a large mound of earth, 30cm high and more than 1m in diameter. The nest itself is a ball of grass and leaves.

The extensive network of shallow burrows can often be seen as ridges running along the surface, while the mole's secondary system of deeper hunting burrows is revealed by the small piles of earth pushed to the surface all over the field (see opposite).

A mole can be studied in captivity for a short time but it needs a large earth-filled box, a supply of water, and a huge amount of food. If his food stock runs out late in the evening he probably will not live until morning so you *must* make sure he is well supplied.

Moles can be caught during ploughing, or when root crops are being lifted, but you must be quick – they can "dive" out of sight in a few seconds. To avoid bites, hold him firmly round the body, just behind the front legs.

Field vole or field mouse

Field voles are common in meadowland and damp grassland but may also be found in woodland margins, parks and gardens. They feed mainly on the green stems of grasses and their feeding signs are very characteristic (see opposite). A little path is often worn around the base of a grass tuft or bunch of rushes. The stems are bitten off near the ground and pieces carried a short distance away, where they are then gnawed.

In severe winters field voles may cause damage to young plantation conifers and to apple trees by gnawing off the bark in a ring around the base of the trunk. These tiny animals also do a good deal of damage even in the summer months but at this time of year the vole does not eat the bark but instead gnaws away the thin growth layer of the tree which is uncovered as the bark is stripped off.

The field vole has a system of underground burrows, some of which are used as food stores, but the burrows are also connected to a maze of little surface pathways hidden under the grass. These "runs" are completely covered and can usually only be seen if you part the grass over them (see opposite). The

Mole

It uses its claws to control its prey – earthworms ▼

▲ Mole-hills from deeper burrows

Ridges made by surface runs ▼

Field vole

Marshy grassland with herbs and tussock grass

Green stems of rushes are eaten but white pith ▼ is discarded

◄ Nest

Runs with grass removed ▼

Harvest mouse

It uses all ► four feet and its tail to climb

The breeding nest ▲ hangs between wheat stalks

female makes her little domed nest of woven grass just off one of the runs, sometimes under the additional cover of a hedgerow root or fallen branch.

Harvest mouse

This remarkable little acrobat is the smallest British mammal apart from the pygmy shrew and in its physical adaptations and behaviour it is perfectly suited to life amongst tall grassy vegetation.

It usually feeds by climbing the grass stem, stealing the seeds from the "ear" at the top, then carrying them down to ground level to eat them. At various times of the year the mouse will also take berries, growing plant shoots, and a variety of grubs and larvae. Like many small animals it uses up its energy very quickly and therefore the day is taken up with alternating periods of feeding and resting.

The nest is a sphere of interwoven grass leaves, plaited together after being stripped lengthwise into fine strands. It is made from the living grass and is green when fresh but usually fades to brown in the autumn. The breeding nest (shown above) is larger and more strongly made than the rather loosely-woven sleeping nest.

In close-up the harvest mouse is fascinating. Its tiny feet, both front and back, are adapted for grasping, and the last 2cm of the tail is prehensile – that is, it can be coiled round a stem to act almost as a fifth "hand".

173

Only a high seat will enable you to escape detection by the returning adult as it circles round the den, checking it from every side

Wind direction

Cubs love to play, especially in the early morning and early evening, but they soon learn to be wary of intruders

▲ **Not even the hardest tree seat can spoil the thrill of watching a family of wild foxes.**

Red fox

Unlike the badger, who uses the same home throughout the year, the dog fox and vixen come together only during the breeding season. From July until March the animals live alone, and their movements are quite unpredictable. The pair mate in winter and the cubs are born in April or May in a den or "earth" excavated in the side of a bank. Very often the fox will take over a rabbit burrow and enlarge it, and on several occasions foxes have been seen sharing the same burrow complex with a badger family.

The fox's territory usually covers a variety of habitats including farmland with hedges and ditches, open country, scrubland and some woodland. If you make careful notes each time a fox is seen or heard in the area a pattern will soon emerge and this will give a clear idea of the animal's territory and favourite routes. Early in the spring you can look for signs of an occupied den and a number of

unmistakable field signs will tell you whether or not a burrow is occupied by foxes. Firstly there is the strong smell – quite unlike that of any other animal you are likely to meet. Secondly the fox is a messy housekeeper and the ground around the entrance will be littered with the remains of its prey – feathers, bones and bits of fur – and with droppings. These can be quite interesting in themselves. In summer, foxes eat a lot of berries and their droppings become stained with the juices, but when animal prey is the main food the high proportion of bone in the food makes the droppings white or grey.

The best fox-watching period is May to June when the youngsters are tied to the earth, usually guarded by the vixen while the dog is away hunting. As the cubs get older the parents leave them for short spells and then you can often creep up to quite close range – as long as you approach carefully from downwind.

If the parents are away you can climb into a tree nearby and wait for their return. And here you will see just how wary the adult fox is. Instead of making a direct approach to the den, the returning fox will circle round, checking the wind for any sign of trouble and finally coming in from directly down-wind. That is why it is important to get well above ground. Once the vixen scents danger she will bark a warning to her cubs to get underground, and she will move the family to a new home at the very first opportunity.

Stoats and weasels

If ever you see a rabbit frozen to the spot, or running along a woodland path looking dazed, freeze absolutely still at once. You may then see one of nature's most ruthless hunters in action. The glazed look is fright, and following close behind, in no great hurry, will be the rippling, bounding shape of a stoat. Before many more minutes have passed the stoat will pounce, putting the rabbit out of its misery with one quick bite at the back of the head.

Stoats and weasels are among the most elusive and difficult animals to watch. They are small, slender, very quick in their movements and very agile so you must make the very best of every chance meeting. If you come across a stoat crossing a country road, stop and remain quite still. The animal will vanish into cover in a flash – but will then reveal one of its most delightful characteristics. Within a few seconds, curiosity will get the better of it and its head will pop up as it takes a long hard look at *you* with its piercing black eyes before vanishing again from sight.

▲ A stoat in its summer coat: the tip of its tail is always black, unlike that of the weasel.

Like most predatory mammals, stoats and weasels love to chase and wrestle, especially when young, and if you are lucky enough to spot a breeding den in a hole in a wall, or in a hollow tree or an old rabbit burrow, then careful watching will bring huge rewards.

The weasel is like a small version of the stoat, very tiny, and slender enough to follow mice right into their holes. Like its larger relative it is a ferocious hunter and because it burns up so much energy it must eat about one-third of its own weight in food each day. Despite its small size – no more than 22cm long with a 6cm tail – the weasel will tackle animals as large as rabbits and, much more impressively, full-grown rats. Apart from the difference in size, and slight differences in colouring, the main difference between the two animals shows itself in winter when, in the northern part of its range, the stoat turns silvery white but for the jet black tip to its tail. In this form it is known as ermine.

175

Life of the hedgerow

Like a vast lattice criss-crossing the countryside, spanning valleys and encircling moors and mountains, the hedge is, surprisingly, mainly a man-made structure. Varying greatly in size and shape, the vast majority of hedges were planted to form field boundaries and enclosures although a few are the sad remains of former woodland margins. These woodland relics can often be identified by combinations of typical woodland plants – dog's mercury, primrose, bluebell and hazel among them.

As more and more woodland disappears from the countryside, the hedges become increasingly important as places of shelter and as foraging grounds for many animals. But even the hedges are under constant pressure. Modern agriculture demands large open fields, not a patchwork of small ones, and recent years have seen thousands of miles of mature hedgerow ripped out in the name of efficiency.

Robin in threat posture

Songposts

▲ The robin, a familiar hedgerow bird, becomes noisy and aggressive at the start of the breeding season. The males broadcast their claims to their chosen territory by singing loudly from well-placed songposts.

See if you can identify these songposts on several visits to the same area, marking them on a map.

Residents and visitors

In addition to the small mammals like the shrew, bank vole and wood mouse, the hedge provides nesting and feeding niches for a great many birds from resident blackbirds, finches and dunnocks to visiting fieldfares and redwings. The insect and spider population is enormous, with beetles, butterflies, moths, bugs, crickets and flies of all kinds providing another rich source of food for predatory birds and mammals. Reptiles and amphibians also make their homes in the banks at the foot of the hedge.

Other animals use the hedge as a routeway or as temporary cover. A sparrowhawk, for example, will often fly fast and low close to a hedge or woodland edge, remaining hidden until it suddenly swerves into view to pounce on some unsuspecting small bird. Songbirds make use of convenient posts and trees in a hedge for warning off rivals. Many butterflies also use the still air in the lee of a hedge when migrating across country, following the line of the hedge whenever it lies roughly in the right direction.

Studies along a hedgerow

The age of a hedge can be estimated from the number of different species of shrub and tree it contains. Pace out a length of 30 metres, and count the species. Allowing 100

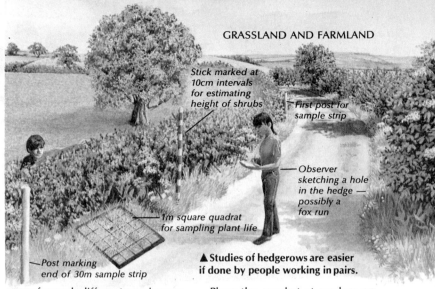

Stick marked at 10cm intervals for estimating height of shrubs

First post for sample strip

Observer sketching a hole in the hedge — possibly a fox run

1m square quadrat for sampling plant life

Post marking end of 30m sample strip

▲ **Studies of hedgerows are easier if done by people working in pairs.**

years for each different species you see, you can then estimate roughly the age of the hedge, by taking an average over several sample sections. Five or six hundred years is by no means rare. At the same time, you could measure all the shrubs in the hedge and identify them. Use a post to judge their height (see above).

The vegetation on both sides of the hedge is also worth studying; you could compare the hedgerow vegetation found on one type of soil with that found on another type. Rather than laboriously count every specimen and every species along the whole hedgerow, you can use a "sampling" technique which cuts down the area of study to one square metre.

To do this, you need to make a grid, or "quadrat" as shown on this page. It consists of a wooden frame, one metre square, divided up into smaller segments by pieces of cotton or string. Your record sheet should be drawn up showing the same number of small segments.

Place the quadrat at random on areas whose vegetation you wish to study, then mark on your record sheet the position and number of different plants that fall within the quadrat. If, for example, daisies occur in ten of the small segments in one random search, but in only two segments in another area, this fact should be noted: it may point to a different type of vegetation in the second area. A sample taken in this way on a wet area will yield quite a different plant "profile" from one taken in a dry area: what other factors might influence vegetation?

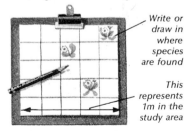

Write or draw in where species are found

This represents 1m in the study area

Divide your record sheet into segments, just like the quadrat.

Spiderwatch

Folklore and tradition have not been kind to spiders. Like sharks and snakes they are widely disliked and even feared by many people, and yet this seems rather unfair for not only are spiders very useful but they are also among the most fascinating of creatures. One of our leading experts has estimated that a single acre of undisturbed meadow may have a spider population of well over two million. Think of how many more flies there would be without these busy and efficient predators.

Some spiders are adapted to life in wet conditions, others to dry: some can tolerate low temperatures while others must keep warm: some hunt by day while others are active in the hours of darkness. The web-spinners feed mainly on flying insects, or make snares to catch running or creeping insects, but the free-ranging hunters use various chase and ambush methods to capture their prey.

Looking for spiders

Their generally dull colouring and very small size make spiders quite difficult to see, but many can be located by looking for their delicate and intricate snares.

The best time to look for web-makers is early in the morning with the dew still glistening, or after a light shower of rain. Move forward slowly, if possible towards the sun so that the webs catch the light and so that your shadow does not fall across the web. Spiders have poor eyesight except at extremely close range, but a sudden shadow spells danger – often from an attacking bird – and is the signal to dash for cover.

When you get close to a web,

check carefully for long radiating strands. These threads are sometimes quite long and if you break one the spider will be on the alert. To lure a spider into the open, try the tuning fork trick (page 152) or select a very fine feathery grass stem and touch it against the web with a trembling movement. The spider makes up for its limited vision by being extremely sensitive to vibration and most species dash out to investigate a possible "catch".

To sample spider populations you can lay a sheet below a small bush and give it a good shake, or make up a strong version of a butterfly net and sweep it across long grass in a meadow or marsh. Best of all read about the different types (some are described on the opposite page) because once you know their habits, the sooner you will be able to discover for yourself the secrets of their remarkable life-styles.

Garden (or cross) spider

Questions to ask

Locate a garden spider and watch it closely for as long as possible. What insects does it catch? How does it deal with them? Which does it eat, and how many? Does it reject any? Where does it lie in wait?

Make a tear in the web and watch how the spider repairs it. Which parts of the web does the spider walk on? Are they different from the "snare" regions? Look for a spider beginning a new web and see if you can work out the sequence of movements as the web takes shape.

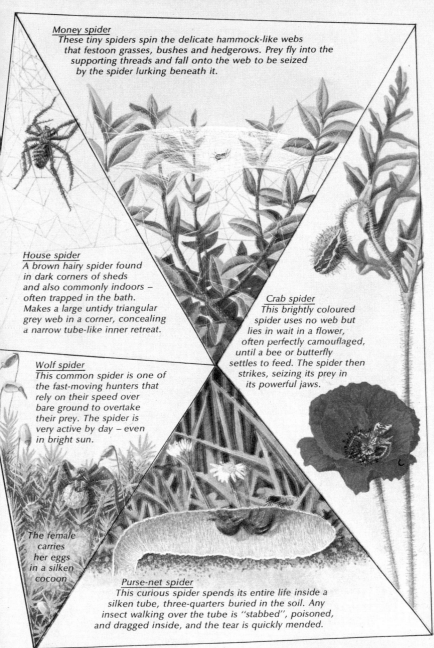

Money spider
These tiny spiders spin the delicate hammock-like webs that festoon grasses, bushes and hedgerows. Prey fly into the supporting threads and fall onto the web to be seized by the spider lurking beneath it.

House spider
A brown hairy spider found in dark corners of sheds and also commonly indoors – often trapped in the bath. Makes a large untidy triangular grey web in a corner, concealing a narrow tube-like inner retreat.

Crab spider
This brightly coloured spider uses no web but lies in wait in a flower, often perfectly camouflaged, until a bee or butterfly settles to feed. The spider then strikes, seizing its prey in its powerful jaws.

Wolf spider
This common spider is one of the fast-moving hunters that rely on their speed over bare ground to overtake their prey. The spider is very active by day – even in bright sun.

The female carries her eggs in a silken cocoon

Purse-net spider
This curious spider spends its entire life inside a silken tube, three-quarters buried in the soil. Any insect walking over the tube is "stabbed", poisoned, and dragged inside, and the tear is quickly mended.

179

Amphibians and reptiles

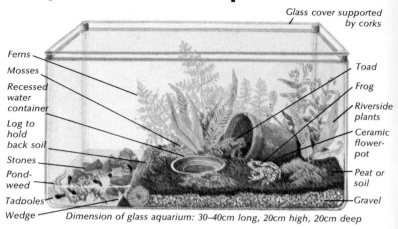

Glass cover supported by corks

Ferns
Mosses
Recessed water container
Log to hold back soil
Stones
Pond-weed
Tadpoles
Wedge

Toad
Frog
Riverside plants
Ceramic flower-pot
Peat or soil
Gravel

Dimension of glass aquarium: 30–40cm long, 20cm high, 20cm deep

Amphibians

Frogs and toads are tied to water during part of their life cycle but are land-dwelling for a large part of the time. In the breeding season (mainly February and March or later for the common frog; mainly March and April for the common toad), frogs and toads congregate at ponds and lakes to mate and spawn. They can be found at night by torch-light if you walk quietly around a suitable spot.

Both these amphibians call to their mates before breeding, so on a warm, damp night, at the appropriate time of year, you could explore local ponds for the animals or their spawn. A tape recorder with a directional microphone (see page 148) will enable you to record their croakings.

Because their skin has a coating of mucus, and also because it damages easily, frogs and toads should be handled as little as possible. If you want to transfer them to a container, catch them with a net.

▲ Vivarium for a common frog or toad. It is best to keep one of these amphibians for not more than six months (from about April), and then to return it to the place where you found it.

A small amount of spawn can be introduced into such a vivarium. If you keep only an adult, however, the "pond" area is not essential – keep the contents moist by spraying regularly with a plant mister. Site the vivarium in a cool but light spot, avoiding intense sunlight.

At home, you can observe common species in a suitable vivarium made from a glass aquarium, as shown above. Provide the frog or toad with sufficient food (live insects, worms or maggots from an angling shop), and let it take what it needs. Feed young tadpoles on algae found on waterweeds, and small aquatic life found in pond-water. Older tadpoles can be fed on small worms and tubifex (from an angling shop). Return the young frogs or toads to the pond where you

Tracks and signs of snakes are ▶ very difficult to detect, and they leave virtually no droppings. However, you may find an empty skin. Snakes shed their skin several times during the year as they grow larger. The process of shedding the old skin is known as "sloughing".

The best time to look for sloughed-off skins is April, when there isn't too much vegetation to hide them. Look around gorse or bramble bushes – the adder rubs itself on thorny sticks to help loosen the skin. If you find one, notice how even the covering for the eyes comes off with the rest of the skin.

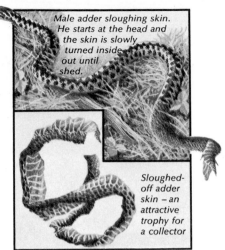

Male adder sloughing skin. He starts at the head and the skin is slowly turned inside out until shed.

Sloughed-off adder skin – an attractive trophy for a collector

found the spawn.

Newts are less easy to find than frogs or toads. However, you may spot an adult at night during the late spring or early summer near a pond, with the aid of a torch.

Lizards

The most commonly-found lizard in this country is the legless slow-worm. It can be distinguished from a snake by the regular size of the scales on its back and stomach (snakes have scales of varying sizes on their body). The slow-worm can often be found under pieces of old metal in gardens, or along disused railway banks.

Many other species of lizard occur in continental Europe and some can be attracted by bait put down in a place where they have already been seen: for some reason, they seem to favour bananas!

Lizards, if handled, should be touched only very gently, and *never* held by the tail: in many species it will come away at the slightest pull.

Snakes

In Britain we have only one poisonous snake – the adder (see above). Its bite is very rarely fatal but it is very painful. In continental Europe there are many more venomous snakes, but, like the adder, none of them will do any harm if they are left alone and observed quietly from a safe distance. A snake sunning itself on a rock is to be watched, admired, photographed: a beautiful animal both at rest and in motion, but one that should not be handled.

Adders are more easily found than our other native snakes – the grass snake and the smooth snake – and April or May is the best time to look. Choose a clear, still, sunny morning that is not too hot. Search in quiet spots on heathland, downland, hedgerows or woodland edges. Walk very softly (snakes can detect footfall easily; however, they will not be able to hear you talk). Carefully check sunny banks that face south or east. Listen, too, for the sound of a snake slithering away into the undergrowth.

181

LIFE OF THE RIVER

The riverbank mammals

Otter

Sadly, otters are now among our less common animals and any observer who manages to watch one will have scored quite a success. They occur mainly in areas that are relatively undisturbed by man – in quiet river valleys, in remote uplands dotted with streams and tarns, and in the wet lowlands of eastern England. They are nocturnal by habit and may sometimes be caught in the headlights of a car while out hunting, but most "observations" consist of their tracks and other signs.

Otters are great travellers and often make long journeys both by river and across country. They are found from the coast, hunting along the shore for shallow-water fishes, crabs and shellfish, right up to the rushing headwaters of mountain streams. In highland regions otters will often cross miles of bleak upland in order to move from one river valley to another. Although beautifully adapted to life in the water, they can move surprisingly quickly on land, usually with a

supple bounding movement that leaves a very distinctive trail (especially on snow-covered ground).

During the day the otter lies up in thick vegetation, often in a reed-bed but occasionally on a low branch or in the crown of a pollarded willow. These temporary resting places are called "hovers". Only when the otter bitch has cubs with her does she use anything like a permanent home. This takes the form of a den called a "holt", dug out of the river bank and usually overhung by vegetation or hidden among the roots of a tree. The entrance is often underwater.

Among the clearest signs that otters are present are their droppings – called "spraints". These are black and rather slimy when fresh, with a strong oily smell. They are often placed on prominent stones, tree stumps or grassy tussocks so that they act as territory markers. The otter's footprint is distinctive although the web between the toes shows clearly only in snow or soft mud. Like many mammals, otters are playful and they seem very fond of

Fish bones and scales, or crab shells, mark an otter's feeding place ▼

◄ Otter cubs love to wrestle and chase each other

◄ An otter's "slide"

A swimming otter leaves a characteristic V-shaped wake ▼

sliding. Grassy or earth banks on favourite routes often show the deep furrow mark of an otter slide, (see below, opposite) and these "toboggan runs" are especially common when there is snow.

Water vole

The smaller riverside mammals are much easier to watch than the secretive otter, particularly as they are active during the day.

The water vole can be found on most stretches of quiet, slow-running river or stream and also along canal banks. These appealing little animals prefer tall riverside banks with plenty of lush vegetation in which they can forage for food, and a careful search will often reveal small patches of vegetation where the plant stems have been neatly bitten off. The water vole's riverbank burrow is easy to identify because the vegetation has usually been grazed for several centimetres all round the entrance.

Your first sign of a water vole is quite likely to be a sound rather than a sight of the animal – a loud "plop" as it makes a dive into the safety of the water having heard you

approaching. If this happens, find a comfortable position in the shade, against a tree or bank that will hide your outline, and wait quietly. The vole will usually reappear within a few minutes and carry on unconcerned.

Water shrew

Like the water vole, the water shrew is short-sighted and is easy to watch as long as you make no loud noises. It is extremely agile in the water, chasing bugs and beetles on the surface, sometimes jumping out of the water to snap up a flying insect, then diving down to walk along the river bed looking for caddis-fly larvae and other small creatures. Its thick fur is dark grey or brown above and silver-grey underneath and holds a lot of air so the animal has a characteristic silvery appearance under water. The water shrew does not hibernate, and in winter a lucky observer may see one hunting under the ice on a frozen stream or pond. The burrow is quite shallow although a deeper hole, lined with soft moss, is usually made as a nursery for the young during the summer breeding season.

◄ The water vole has a blunt face, very tiny ears, and a furry tail

◄ Close-cropped grass reveals the entrance to a water vole burrow

◄ A network of runs fans out from the water vole's burrow

A hunting water shrew streaks after a large pond skater ►

Freshwater life

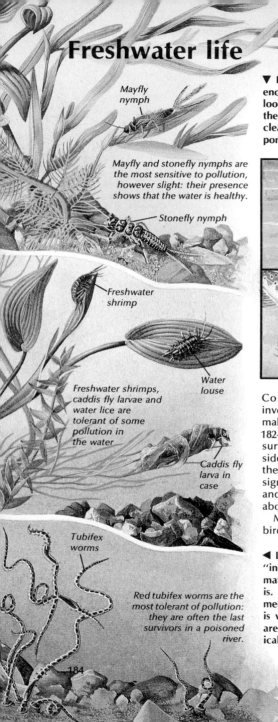

Mayfly nymph

Mayfly and stonefly nymphs are the most sensitive to pollution, however slight: their presence shows that the water is healthy.

Stonefly nymph

Freshwater shrimp

Water louse

Freshwater shrimps, caddis fly larvae and water lice are tolerant of some pollution in the water

Caddis fly larva in case

Tubifex worms

Red tubifex worms are the most tolerant of pollution: they are often the last survivors in a poisoned river.

184

▼ Polarizing sunglasses make an enormous difference when you are looking at a water surface. Almost all the surface glare is removed, giving a clear view of the bed of the stream or pond.

Countless plants, fishes and invertebrates, as well as the mammals already mentioned (on pages 182–3) depend on fresh water for survival. A patient riverside or pool-side observer will need to look for these creatures and the clues or signs of their presence not only in and on the water, but also in the air above it and along the banks.

Most freshwater areas are rich in birdlife – ducks, geese, kingfishers,

◀ Look for these animals (known as "indicators") in fresh water to esti-mate how polluted or clean the water is. If they are all present, including members of the first group, the water is very clean. Some rivers, however, are so full of waste and harmful chem-icals that nothing can live in them.

A simple home-made underwater viewer cuts out the glare of reflected sunlight and the distortion caused by ripples. Remove the top and bottom of a large tin and fix clear plastic film over one end. Place the "window" end in the water and look through the open end, if necessary using your hands as blinkers to cut out light from the sides.

herons, coots and moorhens being the most easily found. There are also those fascinating animals whose lives are spent partly in the water and partly out. Many go through egg and nymph stages in the water before emerging to spend their adult lives at the surface or flying above it.

Where to look

The richest habitats for freshwater life are the lower reaches and estuaries of the river, for here the broad, meandering stretches of water lie between banks crowded with vegetation, and the slow-moving water contains a varied and plentiful supply of food. Higher up the river, in the hills where it has its source, the rushing mountain torrent holds very few species: the trout (above left) has the oxygen-rich waters almost to itself.

If you are lucky enough to be near a lowland stream that is unpolluted, the technique shown above for looking under the water surface will prove useful. Don't, however, try this on the banks of a big river – you might fall in.

The main pollutants of freshwater are chemical wastes from industrial processes, untreated sewage, and hot water from power stations, and the most affected areas are the larger, slow-moving rivers.

Certain animals act as indicators of the purity of the water (see illustrations on the opposite page), so you could gain an impression of how clean your local river or stream really is by searching for these species.

SHORE LIFE

The narrow strip of land we call the seashore is one of the most fascinating habitats on earth. It can vary in just a few miles from gently sloping sandy beaches backed by sand dunes or saltmarshes, to huge areas of mud-flats that are swamped by the sea at every tide, or to jagged rocks reaching out into the sea from the foot of towering cliffs.

Each of these habitats is home to a vast number of highly specialized animals and plants, many of which are not found in any inland habitat. On the shore we can see a succession of "life zones", each of which harbours animals that are adapted to the particular conditions of that environment. All the seashore zones are compressed into a band often as little as 100 metres wide.

The outer edges of this band are marked by the low-water line, beyond which the shore is permanently under water, and the high-water mark where the land really begins. One of the most interesting studies is to take a strip, say a metre wide, from above the high-water mark to beyond the low-water mark and to examine all the different life-forms it contains – finding out just how each one is suited to life in its own part of the beach.

Beachcombing
Above the high-water mark is the strand line – a stretch of seaweed thrown up by the tides; rubbish; empty shells of molluscs and crustaceans (such as crabs); driftwood; bones and egg cases of various fishes (such as the dogfish), and other such collectable items. Within this beachcomber's paradise are the living creatures that benefit from any available food sources – tiny sand-

Observer inside a seaweed-draped canvas bag

▲ **Rock pools, sand dunes and sandy beaches are among the habitats that the naturalist can explore.**

hoppers, flies, and larger animals like gulls and turnstones that pick off tiny shellfish, or worms and other organisms that are clinging to the weed or bits of wood.

This is one of the more accessible areas of the beach to explore for wildlife, along with rock pools, for these are self-contained mini-habitats within the larger area of the shore.

Birdwatching
For millions of wading birds and wildfowl the great river estuaries provide an unfailing source of food – especially in winter when huge flocks of birds travel south from their northern breeding grounds to over-winter in warmer parts of the world.

Their activities are governed by the tides and for birdwatchers the best time of day is usually about two hours before high tide. As the tide surges up the estuary, worms and all kinds of molluscs emerge from their burrows to feed on the rich supply of food carried in the water, and as the tide rises higher the birds become

Use a net to catch marine creatures in a rock pool – but don't let your shadow fall on the surface

A quadrat makes it easy to compare sample areas from different dunes

more and more concentrated in a narrow band.

The birdwatcher can also find plenty of species to study on a rocky or sandy beach, but in these habitats every trick of self-concealment is needed to get close to the birds. On rocky shores, make careful use of the cover available from the rocks themselves, but on open, sandy beaches, you may need to resort to the method shown above and lie in wait, hidden in a camouflaged canvas bag that disguises your tell-tale shape. This method obviously requires patience, as well as care in getting into position without causing too much disturbance. Check out the beach you have chosen for footprints of birds before you decide on the best spot.

Behind the beach

Areas of sand dunes and shingle will often be used by gulls and terns for their simple scraped nests, but dune areas in particular may also contain familiar heath birds such as skylarks and wheatears. When you are exploring dunes, watch out for well-camouflaged eggs that are easily crushed underfoot, and try to avoid known breeding areas during the nesting season – it may disturb the birds.

Sand dunes and saltmarshes offer far more than just birdlife. Here again the specialists thrive and the plant kingdom and insect worlds provide a wealth of interest for the naturalist, and opportunities for making field observations.

A dune survey of plant life can also be carried out using a quadrat (see page 177). What species are present? How are the plants adapted to their constantly shifting environment? For a longer-term project choose a recently-formed dune (one on which relatively few species have become established) and plot its progress over the months or years.

Cliffs

Millions of seabirds lay their eggs on precarious cliff-ledges, safe from ground predators and free from disturbance by man. For similar reasons, grey seals will favour caves and beaches hidden away at the foot

187

LIFE ON THE SHORE

of steep cliffs or on remote rocky islands. The best way to spot these birds and mammals is therefore from a boat, accompanied by someone with local knowledge of the animals' haunts.

The heath-like habitat along the cliff top is home to many interesting wild flowers and insects (including butterflies), and here too the naturalist may find reptiles, birds such as the stonechat, and even larger mammals like the fox.

Play it safe

The coast is no place for taking chances. Never walk far out on mud-flats unless you know the area very well. At the very best you may lose your wellingtons in the sticky mud. By the same token it is foolish to go out on a low rocky headland without keeping a careful watch on the incoming tide – and on your route back to the beach. Finally, never try to look over a cliff: cliff-top winds swirl in all directions, and if you *are* near enough to look over the edge it is more than likely that you will be standing on an overhang – and this could give way under your weight at any moment.

Coast watch

Every year thousands of tons of litter – plastic bottles, drinks cans, bits of metal, plastic and wood – are washed ashore on our beaches. This mountain of rubbish gets little publicity compared with the outcry that follows an oil spill, and yet it grows day by day, piled up by each incoming tide. It is unpleasant to look at, it causes injuries, threatens wildlife and occasionally it can pose a very serious threat to health. More than once, rusting or punctured containers have come ashore leaking dangerous chemicals.

Problems must be properly understood before they can be solved. And that is where you can help; by joining in the **National Shoreline Litter and Refuse Survey**. It is quite straightforward. You can do it alone, with your family, or through your school. It can be done occasionally, during weekend or holiday visits to the coast or, if you live near the sea, you can make a regular survey of a chosen study area. Every single survey form filled in provides valuable information, and hard facts are the best weapons in the fight against pollution of the sea.

How to join in

If you want to find out more, write to the Keep Britain Tidy Group, Bostel House, 37 West Street, Brighton BN1 2RE. (Special information sheets are available for school teachers and youth leaders.)

WHERE TO FIND OUT MORE

Before setting out to watch animals in the wild, it is worth visiting a zoo or wildlife park. There, wary animals like deer can be studied at leisure. Make good use also of your local museum, looking at animal specimens (see page 111). Nature trails and reserves run by organizations such as the National Trust, the County Naturalist Trusts, the RSPB and the main National Parks, provide a "half-way" stage between books and museums, and doing fieldwork on your own.

Clubs

Please remember to enclose a self-addressed stamped envelope whenever you write to a society asking for information.

County Naturalists' Trust. You can get the address of your local Trust from the Royal Society for Nature Conservation, 22 The Green, Nettleham, Lincoln LN2 2NR. They will also give you information about the WATCH club — the junior branch of the Nature Conservation Trusts. WATCH has its own magazine, projects and local groups.

County or Local Natural History Societies. You can get the address of your local Society from CoEnCo, Zoological Gardens, Regents Park, London NW1. They plan programmes of talks and outings each year.

The Mammal Society. For information about youth membership write to: Ms Lenton, 5 St. Stephens Court, Bath, Avon.

The Amateur Entomologists' Society has younger members as well as adults. Write to: 355 Hounslow Road, Hanworth, Feltham, Middlesex.

The Wildfowl Trust, like the RSPB, owns several reserves. For details about junior membership write to: Membership Secretary, The Wildfowl Trust, Slimbridge, Gloucestershire.

Books

A Field Guide to the Mammals of Britain and Europe by F. H. Van Den Brink (Collins). Also in that series, **Birds of Britain and Europe, Wild Flowers, Trees, Insects, Mushrooms,** etc. and the very useful **Guide to Animal Tracks and Signs** by Bang and Dahlstrom.

Finding and Identifying Mammals in Britain by G. B. Corbet (BMNH).

David Stephen's Guide to Watching Wildlife (Collins).

For younger readers the **Usborne Spotters Guides** provide simple, clear field-guide information.

First Guide to Cameras and Photographs by P. Hawksby (Usborne).

A Wildlife Photographers' Code of Practice (RSPB).

Collecting from Nature by T. J. Jennings (Wheaton).

A Handbook for Naturalists Mark Seaward (Constable).

Wild Life in the Garden by T. J. Jennings (Pergamon).

The Amateur Naturalist's Handbook by V. Brown (Faber).

Field Natural History by Alfred Leutscher (Bell).

Studying Insects by R. L. Ford (Warne).

A range of cassette recordings of British bird-songs, and video recordings of birdlife, is available from the RSPB (see page 126).

See also pages 60–2 and pages 126–7 for further useful addresses and books.

INDEX

Where a subject is illustrated, the page number appears in *italics*.